DRIVING STANDARDS AGEN

C000300313

THE OFFICIAL DSA

Guide for Driving Instructors

DRIVING SKILLS

London: The Stationery Office

Published by The Stationery Office

Published with the permission of the Driving Standards Agency on behalf of the Controller of Her Majesty's Stationery Office

Applications for reproduction should be made in writing to The Copyright Unit, Her Majesty's Stationery Office, St Clements House, 2–16 Colegate, Norwich NR3 1BQ

ISBN 0 11 551785 5

A CIP catalogue record for this book is available from the British Library

Other titles in the Driving Skills series
The Official Theory Test for Car Drivers and Motorcyclists
The Official Theory Test for Drivers of Large Vehicles
The Driving Test
The Driving Manual
The Bus and Coach Driving Manual
The Motorcycling Manual
The Theory Test and Beyond (CD-ROM)

The Driving Standards Agency (DSA) would like to thank its staff for their efforts in producing this book.

In order to maintain high standards for joining the Register for ADI(Car), periodical changes may be made to the requirements.

The information contained in this publication is for guidance only, and every effort has been made to ensure that it is correct at the time of going to press.

The Stationery Office cannot be held responsible for any inaccuracies.

The Driving Standards Agency (DSA) is an Executive Agency of the Department of the Environment, Transport and the Regions. You'll see its logo at test centres.

The aim of DSA is to promote road safety through the advancement of driving standards.

DSA

- Conducts practical driving tests for drivers or riders of cars, motorcycles, lorries, buses and other vehicles
- Plans, maintains and supervises the theory test for drivers or riders of cars, motorcycles, lorries and buses
- Controls the register of Approved Driving Instructors (Car) (ADIs)
- Controls the voluntary register of LGV Instructors
- Supervises Compulsory Basic Training (CBT) courses for learner motorcyclists
- Aims to provide a high-quality service to its customers.

Section Five — The Check Test

Section Six — Voluntary Code of Practice

Section Seven — Further Information

Taking any examination can be a traumatic experience, especially if you don't fully understand it's structure.

This book has been written and designed to explain the steps you need to take in order to gain access to, and remain on, the Register of Approved Driving Instructors (Car). It's a comprehensive guide to the examination, explaining in detail each aspect that is assessed during each of the tests. It gives a clear insight into the marking system and what the examiners are looking for, and it is an invaluable tool for both prospective and established driving instructors.

DSA aims to promote road safety through the advancement of driving standards. To this end several improvements have been proposed in order to maintain a high standard of driving instruction in Great Britain. These proposals are due to be implemented in October 1998. Future editions of this publication will inform you of any changes made at that time.

Passing the examination and successfully demonstrating retained knowledge during check tests should not be considered all there is to teaching members of the public to drive. Like the L test, the ADI examinations should be the minimum standard and the starting point for further development.

You should not rest on your laurels once on the Register. There are many books, courses and tests to further develop your teaching skills and make your teaching role more enjoyable.

Mike Ambrose
The Registrar of Approved Driving Instructors

ABOUT THIS BOOK

This book has been written as a guide to the process necessary to become an Approved Driving Instructor (Car) (ADI) and to assist those who are already on the register.

One of the aims is to dispel any myths and uncertainties about the ADI qualifying examination and the 'Check Test' – the test of continuing ability and fitness to give driving instruction.

It explains

- the purpose and maintenance of the Register and the role of the Registrar
- the three part qualifying examination for entry onto the Register of Approved Driving Instructors (Car)
- the role of the Driving Standards Agency (DSA) Supervising Examiners for Approved Driving Instructors (SE ADIs)
- the Check Test.

Section One tells you how to get started. It explains about the Register of ADIs and the responsibilities involved in becoming an ADI.

Section Two guides you through your preparation for the written test, explaining the content and its delivery.

Section Three explains how your driving ability will be tested, the standard required and how it is assessed.

Section Four shows you what is expected of you during the instructional technique test. It explains the marking and assessment procedures.

Section Five explains how your continued instructional ability and fitness to instruct (the Check Test) is marked and assessed. It advises on how to prepare yourself fully. As this section also deals with advice on giving instruction, some of the content is similar to Section Four.

Section Six explains the voluntary code of practice for driving instructors.

Section Seven gives further information you might find useful in your chosen profession.

The ultimate aim is to promote

'safe driving for life'

Books for study

The Stationery Office publishes books in the Driving Skills series on behalf of DSA. *The Driving Manual* and *The Driving Test* are highly recommended. *The Highway Code* is, of course, essential for all road users. There are also books about driving available from other publishers.

As you read this book you will see references to other publications approved by DSA. These could be of benefit to you. You can also find a recommended reading list in Section Two.

The topics covered

- The responsibilites of becoming an Approved Driving Instructor (Car)
- The Register of Approved Driving Instructors (Car)
- The role of the Supervising Examiner (SE ADI)
- Preparing for the qualifying examination

The responsibilities of becoming an Approved Driving Instructor

Have you given serious thought to what is involved? You may have considered some of the advantages and the attraction of being self-employed, possibly driving a new car, having your own business and a professional status, but before going any further it is just as important to consider the challenges which lie ahead.

If you qualify you will become a member of a relatively small group of people who have the qualities and knowledge to teach a very worthwhile skill. You will have earned the status of being a true professional through many hours of study and practical training.

As a professional you will be considered an expert in your field. The work of an ADI can be very satisfying and rewarding. It's a good feeling to see your pupil waving a pass certificate after the test knowing you have taught them well, and to have the satisfaction of knowing that you are making a worthwhile contribution towards road safety.

However, teaching people to drive isn't an easy job. You must be prepared for a lot of hard work, and the initial training may cost you much time, dedication and money – more than you may think.

Your job will involve mixing with all types of people, some of whom you may not find it easy to get on with. This will demand a lot of patience and understanding.

The nature of the job may require you to work unsociable hours to fit in with your pupils' needs.

You must be able to maintain a very high level of concentration throughout your working day to safeguard yourself, your pupils and other road users. Your last lesson of the day should be conducted with the same enthusiastic approach and competence as your first – and that's difficult.

You may consider starting your own driving school. Having to run your own business in an effective and efficient manner will put extra demands on you and may extend your working day.

Once you have qualified, your continued fitness and ability to give instruction will be checked from time to time, or when required by the Registrar.

DSA and the driving instruction industry place great emphasis on professional standards and business ethics.

A code of practice has been agreed and is the framework within which all instructors should operate. Details of this code can be found in Section Six.

An information pack entitled 'Your Road to Becoming an ADI (Car)', is available from DSA HQ. Tel: 0115 901 2500. This pack also contains a guide to approved training establishments.

The Register of Approved Driving Instructors (Car)

A brief history

The Register was introduced in October 1964 on a voluntary basis.

There have been many changes to its structure over the years, including the qualifying examination syllabus. Today, ADIs are known as Driving Standards Agency Approved Driving Instructors (Car).

Approximately one year later more than 3000 instructors had qualified and could claim the title of being a 'Ministry of Transport Approved Driving Instructor'.

In October 1970 new legislation was introduced. From that date anyone giving paid instruction in cars had to qualify and enter the Register by law.

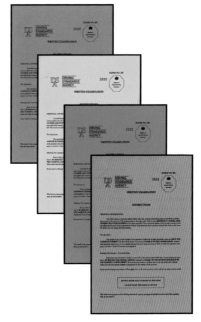

Responsibilities of the Registrar

The Register of Approved Driving Instructors (Car) was set up to operate in the interests of road safety. Its purpose is to maintain and improve the standard of car driving instruction available to the general public.

It ensures that the public can rely on a minimum standard of tuition from registered driving instructors. It is administered by DSA under the provisions of the Road Traffic Act 1988 (as amended).

Under the rules of this Act it is against the law to charge (either money or money's worth) for instruction unless your name is on the Register of Approved Driving Instructors (Car) or you hold a trainee 'Licence to give instruction' issued by the Registrar.

There are exceptions: for example, some employees of

• local authorities

• police forces

whilst on official duty.

The Registrar's responsibilities are to make sure that the standards of service and performance are maintained. This includes

• administration of the Register, which has approximately 33,000 ADIs and 1,500 licensed trainees

• administration of the 'Pass Plus' scheme of 'post test' driver training

• improving the quality of driver training in Great Britain

• developing policy on driver training generally

• keeping the waiting times for practical qualifying tests to a minimum

• issuing test results within given time limits

• offering ADI Check Tests within time limits determined by Grade Assessment

• administration of the Voluntary Register of Large Goods Vehicle (LGV) Trainers

• administration of Compulsory Basic Training (CBT) courses for learner motorcyclists.

Your responsibilities to the Registrar

Any change in your personal circumstances affecting your entitlement to become or remain as an ADI must be reported to the Registrar within seven working days of that change. These include

- any change in your status as a fit and proper person

- any convictions including motoring offences. If this results in a disqualification from driving, you will automatically have to surrender your Certificate of Registration or your trainee licence.

- a change of permanent home or business address
  - your personal records on the Register **must** be updated. If you are unable to be contacted when a Check Test is due, it will eventually result in your removal from the Register

- a decision to cease instruction permanently or for a period of time due to illness or living abroad.

In any of these circumstances you must return your Certificate to the Registrar. If you have any doubts and need guidance, contact your Supervising Examiner (SE ADI).

What powers does the Registrar have?

The Registrar can

- refuse admission to or the right to remain on the Register
  - this is dependent on a person satisfying the legal requirements

- refuse re-admission if previously removed as a result of a Court conviction or Check Test failure
  - an important feature in these requirements is whether a person is 'fit and proper'

- remove an ADI from the Register
  - the decision rests with the Registrar and is based on all convictions not spent under the Rehabilitation of Offenders Act 1974.

Removal from the Register may result from, for example

- court convictions after entering the Register

- failure to meet the standard required in a Check Test

- failure to attend a Check Test without a valid reason.

The right to appeal against any of the Registrar's decisions

You have the right to appeal if you are not satisfied with the Registrar's decision to

- refuse your application for entry onto the Register

- remove your name from the Register

- cancel your existing licence or trainee licence

- refuse to issue a further certificate or trainee licence

You will be notified by post of the Registrar's decision and you have the right to make a representation to the Registrar about it.

If the Registrar does not have a change of mind, you then have the right of appeal to the Secretary of State for the Environment, Transport and the Regions.

The Secretary of State will appoint an Appeal Board to hold an inquiry into the matter. A decision will be made after considering the board's recommendations.

The Secretary of State also has the power, if the decision goes against you, to charge you with the cost of the appeal.

This will not normally happen if your appeal is a reasonable one and is treated seriously.

You can find further information about the appeals procedure in Section Seven of this book.

A booklet containing the appeals procedure will be sent automatically if the Registrar decides to

- refuse your application for registration

- remove your name from the Register

- refuse your trainee licence.

Can anyone apply to become an ADI?

Yes, providing they

- hold a British or Northern Ireland car driving licence or hold a European Union (EU)/ European Economic Area (EEA) licence

- have held that licence for a total of four years out of the past six years prior to entering the Register after qualifying. A foreign driving licence, an automatic car driving licence or a provisional licence held after passing the driving test all count towards the four years

- have not been disqualified from driving at any time in the four years prior to applying to enter the Register

- are a fit and proper person to have their name entered in the Register

- are prepared to accept that all convictions, including motoring offences, still in force (i.e., not spent under the Rehabilitation of Offenders Act 1974) will be taken into account when their suitability is assessed

- pass the Register qualifying examination.

The qualifying examination

The qualifying examination is in three parts.

Part One – The Written Test.

Part Two – The Eyesight and Driving Technique Test.

Part Three – The Instructional Ability Test.

You may have as many attempts as required to pass the Part One test. Once you have passed, it triggers the start of a maximum two-year period to succeed at Parts Two and Three.

The start date is calculated from the date you pass the written test.

You are only allowed three attempts to pass the Part Two tests and three attempts to pass Part Three. If you fail the Part Two test on your third attempt, you must wait until the remainder of the two year period has elapsed before re-applying to take the qualifying examination.

When the two-year period has expired, you must start again at the beginning and re-sit the Part One test and pass it, before further attempting to qualify at Parts Two and Three.

The same rules apply with the Part Three test. If you fail the Part Three on your third attempt, you must wait until the two-year period has expired before re-applying to take the qualifying examination. Likewise, you must start again at the beginning and succeed at the Part One test before moving on to Parts Two and Three.

If you run out of time and do not pass all three tests within the maximum two-year period, you will have to start the whole process again. The two-year period cannot be extended.

Who conducts the qualifying examination?

This specialist area of testing is conducted by experienced and carefully selected driving examiners. It is a very demanding job that requires special skills, particularly in assessment and communication.

Examiners undergo an intensive training course conducted at the DSA's Training Establishment at Cardington in Bedfordshire.

Their work is frequently monitored by SE ADIs and Assistant Chief Driving Examiners who sit in on the tests.

This is to ensure that the standards of marking and assessment are correctly adhered to and the tests are conducted in a uniform manner.

Can someone with a disability qualify?

Yes. If their driving licence is marked with a medical restriction, the details listed must be sent with their initial application.

Under the provisions of the Road Traffic Act 1988 as amended by The Road Traffic (Driving Instruction by Disabled Persons) Act 1993, people

Mobility
Advice and
Vehicle
Information
Service

MAVIS
'O' Wing, Macadam Avenue
Old Wokingham Road
Crowthorne
BERKSHIRE
RG45 6XD
Tel: 01344 661000 (and Minicom)
Fax: 01344 661066

ROAD TRAFFIC ACT 1988 AS AMENDED BY ROAD TRAFFIC (DRIVING INSTRUCTION BY DISABLED PERSONS) ACT 1993

EMERGENCY CONTROL CERTIFICATE
No.

I hereby certify that, in accordance with section 133A of the Road Traffic Act 1988

(Name)...... of
(Address)..
...
...
...

has satisfied the Secretary of State that if an emergency arose while he/she was giving, in such motor car, instruction in the driving of an appropriate motor car, he/she is able to take control of a motor car of a class covered by his/her disabled person's limited driving licence

   a.   without modification *
   b.   with the following modification(s) *

I also further certify that the said (name)...... should undergo a further emergency control assessment after the expiry of ...... months/years from the date of this certificate. *

signed...... (Assessor)
on behalf of the Secretary of State

date ......

You are required to tell the Approved Driving Instructors' Register of the Driving Standards Agency at once if your condition changes (includes any physical or mental condition) which affects, or may in the future affect, your fitness as a driving instructor, if you expect it to last more than three months.

*delete as appropriate

with certain physical disabilities, who are only licensed to drive an automatic vehicle, may take the ADI examination. However, they must be able to demonstrate that they could take control of the steering and brakes from the passenger seat in the event of an emergency.

Such persons should apply to the Mobility Advice and Vehicle Information Service (MAVIS) who will carry out an emergency control assessment.

If this is completed satisfactorily an Emergency Control Certificate (ECC) will be issued. This will state the adaptations which need to be fitted to the vehicle before that person can be allowed to teach. A copy of this certificate will be sent to DSA and the usual ADI qualifying process can then begin.

The requirements for the practical tests – Parts Two and Three of the qualifying examination, are exactly the same as for all other candidates, except that in Part Three – the test of instructional ability – the adaptations listed on the Emergency Control Certificate must be fitted.

The address of MAVIS is

Department of the Environment, Transport and the Regions Mobility Advice and Vehicle Information Service
O Wing
MacAdam Avenue
Old Wokingham Road
Crowthorne
Berkshire
RG45 6XD
Tel: 01344 661000.

The role of the Supervising Examiner (SE ADI)

There are over fifty Supervising Examiners (SE ADIs) throughout Great Britain. Northern Ireland operates a similar Register which is run by the Driver and Vehicle Testing Agency (DVTA).

They are all very highly trained and experienced people and are responsible for carrying out the operational duties of the Register.

These duties can include

- managing their allocated sections of the country

- arranging and conducting ADI Part Two and Three qualifying tests

- supervising and monitoring staff who conduct ADI qualifying tests

- arranging and conducting ADI Check Tests

- reporting illegal instruction and attending Court when required

- visiting driving schools and training organisations to check that ADI/trainee ratios are correct

- inspecting and reporting on ADI Approved Training Establishments

- attending ADI seminars and giving talks and presentations

- conducting Large Goods Vehicle (LGV) practical examinations for the Voluntary Register of LGV Instructors

- responding to correspondence from the public, and ADI matters in general.

SE ADIs can usually be contacted at their office most Fridays. This is their 'surgery day', although other appointments may be made by prior arrangement.

They are available to offer help and advice on any matter regarding the Register or qualifying examination and to offer guidance on instructional techniques.

If you would like to meet the SE ADI to discuss any of these matters, it is advisable to contact them by telephone first (or leave a message on the answer-phone) to book an appointment.

The address and telephone number of the local SE ADI can be found in Section Seven.

Preparing for the qualifying examination

Each qualifying test will require dedication and commitment. If you are studying while still in full-time work you will have to manage your time effectively.

There are several publications on the market which can help you. A list of recommended reading can be found on pages 34–37.

There are individual ADIs and training establishments who advertise professional help. Some offer residential or distance training courses.

A list of approved training establishments is included in the pack 'Your Road to Becoming an ADI (Car)' available from DSA HQ. Tel: 0115 901 2500.

The Driving Standards Agency maintains two national lists of approved training establishments. These voluntary schemes were set up by the driver training industry together with DSA. They are compiled under two directories.

**ADITE – Approved Driving
Instructor Training Establishments**
PO Box 101
Stockport
SK4 4DW
Tel: 0161 443 1611

**DIA–RTE – Driving Instructors
Association Recommended ADI
Training Establishments**
Safety House
Beddington Farm Road
Croydon
CR0 4XZ

Tel: 0181 665 5151

DIA Recommended
Training Establishment

Both ADITE and DIA–RTE offer those seeking training or retraining details of establishments, and their training methods, which have been inspected by DSA and approved by their respective management committees.

Some training establishments appear in both directories. However, the standards applied to both are the same, so you can approach any of the establishments safe in the knowledge that they have been properly assessed.

It is advisable to contact more than one and compare what they have to offer. This will help you to decide which one most suits your particular needs.

Each entry on the list includes the

• name of the establishment

• address and telephone number

• name of the person in control, who may be the owner or the manager.

There is a code against each establishments name (see below). The code is used to indicate the extent of training offered.

If the establishment offers courses which are not listed against their entry, it is likely that these have not yet been approved.

1 =	ADI PART ONE (The Written Test)		**F** =	Full time course
			P =	Part time course
2 =	ADI PART TWO (The Driving Technique Test)		**D** =	Distance learning course
3 =	ADI PART THREE (The Instructional Ability Test)		**A** =	Residential accommodation course
R =	ADI Retraining			

What to look for in a training course

The following is a list of aspects that you should consider before deciding on the type of course that will suit your needs.

- How much is it going to cost?
- What methods of payment are available?
- Does it include books and test fees?
- Is it a complete course or only part?
- Will I receive an assessment of likely training needs before starting the course?
- What happens if I need more than the training that is offered?
- What extra support will I get if I fail and will it cost any more?
- What teaching methods are used – how much of this is distance learning?
- How much is in-classroom; how much is in-car?
- How many others will be in the car with you?
- Is there any provision for extra practice?
- Will I be able to carry on with my existing job whilst training?
- What guarantee is there that there will be a driving school willing to take me as a trainee at the appropriate time?

- What success rate does the trainer have?
- Will I get a refund of fees if I am unable to complete the course, particularly if this is for reasons beyond my control, e.g., sickness?

If you have any doubts, it's advisable to get the answers in writing. Don't sign or pay anything unless you are sure that the course is what you want.

If you are not satisfied and you cannot settle your dispute with the establishment, you should make your complaint to ADITE or DIA–RTE as appropriate.

DSA cannot accept responsibility for the training provided as this is a contractual matter between you and your chosen training organisation.

There are other establishments that offer ADI training but have decided not to join the voluntary scheme.

In this case, neither the industry as a whole nor DSA can say with confidence what their training standards are because they have not been inspected.

There are other establishments which may have been inspected but have not been able to meet the required standard.

You may have been driving for many years and, like most fellow drivers, consider yourself to be very proficient.

However, modern cars are constantly being updated with the latest technology including improved safety features. This, in turn, requires an updated knowledge of modern driving skills and techniques. If you have been driving for some years, you may have developed some poor driving habits that you are not aware of.

Make sure you are well prepared before applying to sit each part of the entry examination. You can do it by yourself, but it is not recommended. The detail and complexity of the subjects are best supported by professional guidance.

The amount of training you will need will depend on your current driving ability. Your trainer should be able to assess this. Selecting a good trainer can ultimately save you time and money.

It is false economy to skimp on training because of the cost. Make sure you are properly prepared.

SECTION TWO | THE WRITTEN TEST

The topics covered

- What you need to know
- About the test
- Recommended reading

This is the first of the three-part qualifying examination to gain entry onto the Register. Passing it triggers the start of the maximum two-year period to succeed at Parts Two and Three.

What you need to know

This written test calls for in-depth subject knowledge and understanding. Questions are based on the following subjects.

- Principles of road safety generally and their application in particular circumstances.

- Techniques of driving a car correctly, safely and courteously.

- Understanding and application of vehicle control and road procedure.

- Recognising hazards and taking proper action.

- Dealing correctly with pedestrians and other road users.

- Use of safety equipment.

- Theory and practice of learning, teaching and assessment.

- Instructional techniques needed to teach a pupil to drive a car (which should include the item immediately above).

- The correction of a pupil's errors.

- Knowledge of the appropriate manner and relationship between instructor and pupil.

- A simple understanding of vehicle adaptations for disabled drivers.

- *The Highway Code.*

- The DSA publication *The Driving Test.*

- Interpretation of the reasons for failure given in the DSA form DL25A – the Driving Test report.

- Knowledge, adequate for the needs of driving instruction, of the mechanics and design of a car.

- The DSA publication *The Driving Manual.*

About the test

Tests are held at a number of centres across the country, usually once a month. Locations and dates are listed at DSA Driving Test Centres and SE ADI offices. Application forms can be obtained by writing to:

Driving Standards Agency
ADI Branch
Stanley House
56 Talbot Street
Nottingham
NG1 5GU

You can also get one from your local SE ADI (see page 172). Applications received at DSA headquarters, Nottingham, are normally processed within two weeks.

The time, date and place of your test will be confirmed by a letter of appointment.

Make sure you bring this letter with you as you will be asked to produce it to the invigilator when you attend. Without it, you may not be able to take the test.

Stanley House
56 Talbot Street
NOTTINGHAM
NG1 5GU

Personal Ref No 226202
Our Reference OMA28
Our Tel No 0115 901 2608
Date 08/12/2000

DRIVING
STANDARDS
AGENCY

'Safe driving for life'

Dear Mr

REGISTER OF APPROVED DRIVING INSTRUCTORS

You are invited to attend the written test which is held at the time and place shown below. Please bring this letter with you. You may not be able to participate in the examination if you cannot show this letter to the supervisor.

You should read the regulations for the conduct of the examination, which are attached.

The fee you paid for this appointment cannot normally be refunded unless you give the office at the above address at least ten clear working days' notice of your inability to attend. The day of cancellation, and the day of examination, cannot be counted as part of the 10 days'. To notify us the details below should be completed and this letter returned. The Agency is generally not prepared to consider a refund of fee (or offer you a further appointment without payment of a further fee) where less than ten working days' notice is given.

If you are unable to attend please return this invitation to the address at the top of the letter immediately. We can then give your place to someone else.

You should also telephone this office before the required 10 days as we cannot be responsible for lost or late mail.

The last date allowed for cancelling this test without loss of fee is SHORT NOTICE

Yours sincerely

for Registrar
Approved Driving Instructors

Time	9:00 am	Place
Date	17/12/2000	

The Theatre
Park Crescent Conference Centre
229 Great Portland Street
London
Wln5hd
Tube: Great Portland Street

Notice of Inability to Attend   DO NOT DETACH

PERSONAL REF NO.

I shall not be able to attend the examination as indicated above.

Would you please arrange for me to attend a subsequent test: 226202
*a. as soon as possible   NAME
*b. not before   (date)   Signature   Date
Address

AD16R(Rev March 96)

*Delete as appropriate

DETR   An executive agency of the
ENVIRONMENT   Department of the Environment,
TRANSPORT   Transport and the Regions
REGIONS

What if I am dyslexic?

It may be possible to make special arrangements for candidates with special needs. Those with reading difficulties or dyslexia are required to provide some form of independent confirmation. Requests should be submitted with the application for the Written Test.

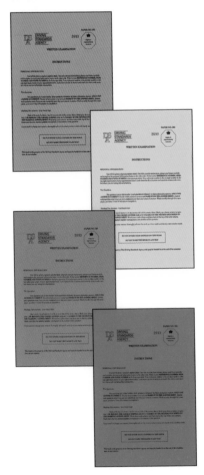

Test fees and refunds

Fees are payable and should be enclosed with each application for the qualifying test.

Your fee will be refunded if you can't keep an appointment for the test, as long as you give at least 10 clear working days notice excluding

- the day of receipt
- the day of the test
- weekends and public holidays.

However, this does not apply to short notice bookings.

You will not receive a refund if

- you do not give enough notice to cancel
- you fail to attend the test through your own fault, e.g., vehicle breakdown on the way.

If you arrive after the test has started you will be advised

- of the time the test began and how late you are
- that you can sit the test in the time remaining
- that no extra time will be allowed if you have not completed the paper when 'time up' is announced.

The written test consists of a single paper with 100 questions.

You should try to answer all of them.

The test takes 90 minutes, but you must allow additional time for the issue of instructions and collection of papers.

The questions from the syllabus are in ten subject groups which are divided into four bands.

The purpose of banding is to ensure candidates have a comprehensive knowledge spread across the whole of the syllabus.

The bands, subject groups and number of questions in each are shown below.

Band 1		
Road procedure	25	questions
Band 2		
Traffic signs and signals	5	questions
Car control	10	questions
Pedestrians	5	questions
Mechanical knowledge	5	questions
Band 3		
Driving test	10	questions
Disabilities	5	questions
Law	10	questions
Band 4		
Publications	10	questions
Instructional techniques	15	questions
Total	100	questions

DRIVING
STANDARDS
AGENCY

Safe driving for life

Stanley House
56 Talbot street
NOTTINGHAM
NG1 5GU

Ms A. D. Isaacs
Acacia Avenue
Diverton
DI 21 7HQ

Pers. Ref No.:123456
20 June 2000

Register of Approved Driving Instructors

Dear Ms Isaacs

I am sorry to tell you that you were not successful in the written part of the qualifying examination for the Register of Approved Driving Instructors. I must inform you therefore that unless you apply to take the examination again no further action will be taken on your application for entry onto the register. The marks you obtained in each band and overall mark are as follows:

BAND AND SUBJECT	MINIMUM BAND PASS MARK	YOUR MARK
	20	24
Band 1 - Road Procedure		25
Band 2 - Traffic Signals and Signs, Car Control, Pedestrians, Mechanics	20	19
Band 3 - Driving Test, Disabilities, Law	20	25
Band 4 - Publications, Instructional Techniques	20	93%
Overall -Examination Pass Mark	85%	

There is no limit to the number of attempts you can make at the written exam and if you decide to sit the written part again, you should fill in the details below and forward the complete letter together with the appropriate fee (cheques etc. should be crossed and made payable to the "Driving Standards Agency") to the above address.

I should explain that you are required to obtain no less than 20 marks in each of the bands as well as the minimum of 85 marks overall in order to pass.

Yours sincerely

for Registrar Approved Driving Instructors

I apply for admission to the written part of the qualifying examination for the Register of Approved Driving Instructors. I enclose the appropriate fee.

Please complete these boxes	Signed
Cheque / P.O. No.	
Daytime Tel No.	Date

How the result is calculated

To pass you must score a minimum of 85%.

This total must include at least 20 correct answers in each band.

A high percentage mark can be scored but still result in failure.

In the example below, the candidate has scored an overall mark of 93% but has failed because the minimum score (20) was not achieved in Band 3 (score: 19).

BAND AND SUBJECT	MINIMUM BAND PASS MARK	YOUR MARK
Band 1 - Road Procedure	20	24
Band 2 - Traffic Signals and Signs, Car Control, Pedestrians, Mechanics	20	25
Band 3 - Driving Test, Disabilities, Law	20	19
Band 4 - Publications, Instructional Techniques	20	25
Overall -Examination Pass Mark	85%	93%

How the questions are set out

You will be given a question book, separate answer sheet and clear guidance notes.

Each question gives you a choice of three answers lettered A, B and C. Only one is correct.

Here are two examples

Question
The publication containing advice to all road users is:

Answers
a. The Driving Manual
b. The book The Driving Test
c. The Highway Code.

Question
What type of road user would use a toucan crossing?

Answers
a. Cyclists and pedestrians.
b. Pedestrians only.
c. Cyclists only.

How to mark the answer sheet

Mark your answer in pencil by circling the appropriate letter – A, B or C – **ONLY ON THE ANSWER SHEET SUPPLIED.**

You should study the questions carefully before deciding which answer is correct. It is a good idea to read them at least twice.

DRIVING
STANDARDS
AGENCY

Register of Approved Driving Instructors
Written Examination

ANSWER SHEET
PAGE 1.

Read the instructions below before you start to fill in the answers.

INSTRUCTIONS

1. Please use a PENCIL.

2. Please complete your name, address and post code details in the boxes provided overleaf using block capital letters.

3. Write your Personal Reference Number in the box provided overleaf.

4. Write the Paper Number in the box provided overleaf.

5. Write your Desk Number in the box provided overleaf.

6. Write the Examination Date in the box provided overleaf.

7. Write the code number of the Test Centre where you are taking the examination in the box provided overleaf

Test Centre	Code Number
Aberdeen	01
Birmingham	02
Bath	03
Cardington	04
Cardiff	05
Not Used	06
Glasgow	07
Leeds	08
Nottingham	09
London	10
Manchester	11
Newcastle-Upon-Tyne	12
Plymouth	13

8. Each question has three possible answers lettered A-C. Select your answer for each question and indicate the answer by putting a circle round the box you have selected as your answer.

Example of completed question.

9. There is only one correct answer for each question. If you circle more than one box for a question, that question will carry no mark.

Printing and processing by Host Data Services Limited, Watford

PAGE 2.

Title | Initials

Surname

Address

Post Code

Personal Reference No.

Date

Desk No.

Paper No.

Test Centre

Column 1

	A	B	C
1	A	B	C
2	A	B	C
3	A	B	C
4	A	B	C
5	A	B	C
6	A	B	C
7	A	B	C
8	A	B	C
9	A	B	C
10	A	B	C
11	A	B	C
12	A	B	C
13	A	B	C
14	A	B	C
15	A	B	C
16	A	B	C
17	A	B	C
18	A	B	C
19	A	B	C
20	A	B	C
21	A	B	C
22	A	B	C
23	A	B	C
24	A	B	C
25	A	B	C

Please go to the top of Column 2

Column 2

	A	B	C
26	A	B	C
27	A	B	C
28	A	B	C
29	A	B	C
30	A	B	C
31	A	B	C
32	A	B	C
33	A	B	C
34	A	B	C
35	A	B	C
36	A	B	C
37	A	B	C
38	A	B	C
39	A	B	C
40	A	B	C
41	A	B	C
42	A	B	C
43	A	B	C
44	A	B	C
45	A	B	C
46	A	B	C
47	A	B	C
48	A	B	C
49	A	B	C
50	A	B	C

Please go to the top of Column 3

Column 3

	A	B	C
51	A	B	C
52	A	B	C
53	A	B	C
54	A	B	C
55	A	B	C
56	A	B	C
57	A	B	C
58	A	B	C
59	A	B	C
60	A	B	C
61	A	B	C
62	A	B	C
63	A	B	C
64	A	B	C
65	A	B	C
66	A	B	C
67	A	B	C
68	A	B	C
69	A	B	C
70	A	B	C
71	A	B	C
72	A	B	C
73	A	B	C
74	A	B	C
75	A	B	C

Please go to the top of Column 4

Column 4

	A	B	C
76	A	B	C
77	A	B	C
78	A	B	C
79	A	B	C
80	A	B	C
81	A	B	C
82	A	B	C
83	A	B	C
84	A	B	C
85	A	B	C
86	A	B	C
87	A	B	C
88	A	B	C
89	A	B	C
90	A	B	C
91	A	B	C
92	A	B	C
93	A	B	C
94	A	B	C
95	A	B	C
96	A	B	C
97	A	B	C
98	A	B	C
99	A	B	C
100	A	B	C

Please see the notes below

Note 1. - Have you marked in pencil your answers in the correct boxes above?
Note 2. - Have you completed your name, address, personal reference number, exam date, desk number, paper number and test centre

Printing and processing by Host Data Services Limited, Watford.

When and how you will be informed of the result

The results are usually sent within two weeks of the test date. If you have not received them within that time, you should contact DSA headquarters.

On the back of the letter informing you of the result there is an application form.

If you pass   you can apply for the Part Two test by completing the form and returning it with the fee to DSA headquarters.

Only do this when you are fully prepared.

If you fail   and want to re-sit the written test, complete the form and return it with the fee to DSA headquarters.

You can re-sit this test as many times as it takes to pass.

Recommended reading

DSA has compiled a list of books
which are recommended to help you
study for the written test. The ISBN
numbers have been included to make
ordering easier.

The Driving Manual

published for DSA by The Stationery
Office
ISBN 0 11 551782 0
Completely up-to-the minute and
easy to understand. Covers everything
the driver needs to know about good
driving techniques for today's
challenging driving conditions.

The Highway Code

published by The Stationery Office
ISBN 0 11 551843 6
Contains important advice for all
road users and encourages one code
of practice for everyone using the
roads to avoid accidents.

The Driving Test

published for DSA by The Stationery Office
ISBN 0 11 551778 2
This remains the only book to include the officially recommended syllabus for learning to drive. This updated edition includes additional information about changes to the test.

DL25A Driving Test Report

This report is issued to all candidates. A very useful document to help ADIs analyse their and their pupils performance. Available from test centres and DSA headquarters.

The Motor Vehicles (Driving Licences) Regulations 1986

ISBN 0 11 063309 1
Contains information about driving licence categories and age limits for different classes of vehicle. It also contains the contents of the theory and practical driving tests.

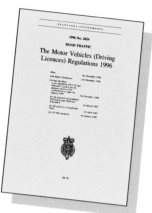

Instructional Techniques and Practice for Driving Instructors

by L.Walklin
published by Stanley Thornes (Publishers) Ltd
ISBN 0 7487 1631 9
Covers in detail the theory and practice of good teaching techniques.
A useful guide purposely written for trainee and qualified ADIs.

The Driving Instructor's Handbook

by J. Miller and M. Stacey
published by Kogan Page.
ISBN 0 7494 1925 3
A reference and training manual for all driving instructors and those studying to become an ADI.

Know Your Traffic Signs

published by The Stationery Office
ISBN 0 11 551612 3
An in-depth book to illustrate and
explain the majority of road signs
and markings that are likely to
be encountered.

You will need to thoroughly
understand the information contained
in these books. They will also be of
great benefit when preparing for the
Part Two and Three tests.

There are other publications
available which you may find useful
for reference.

Once you have passed the Part One
test you have cleared the first hurdle.
You now have a maximum
of two years to successfully
complete Parts Two and Three of the
qualifying examination.

At this point in the qualifying process
you should be well aware of the time,
effort and preparation that is
necessary to succeed.

The topics covered

- Training for the driving technique test
- The eyesight test
- About the test of your driving technique
- How your driving is assessed and marked
- How the overall assessment is made
- The result

Training for the driving technique test

This is the second of the three part qualifying examination to gain entry onto the Register. It consists of an eyesight test and a test of your ability to be able to drive to a very high standard. It will prove whether or not you have a thorough understanding of good safe driving techniques, and that you can also demonstrate them.

This test is far more difficult than the L test. It is of an advanced nature and a very high standard of competence is expected.

As previously mentioned, you have a limit of three attempts at this test.

You must be able to satisfy the examiner in all or any of the following subjects.

- Expert handling of the controls.

- Use of correct road procedure.

- Anticipating the actions of other road users and taking appropriate action.

- Sound judgement of distance, speed and timing.

- Consideration for the convenience and safety of other road users.

- Moving away straight ahead and at an angle.

- Overtaking, meeting or crossing the path of other vehicles, and taking an appropriate course without undue hesitancy.

- Turning left-hand and right-hand corners correctly and without undue hesitancy.

- Stopping the vehicle as in an emergency safely and under full control.

- Reversing into limited openings to the left and right.

- Reverse parking behind a parked vehicle.

- Turning the car to face in the opposite direction using forward and reverse gears.

Where the tests are conducted

The tests are conducted from an SE ADI office during normal office hours Monday to Thursday. The locations are listed in Section Seven.

As with any appointment, allow plenty of time for your journey to the SE's office. If you are not sure where it is, don't leave it to the day of the test to find out.

Tests are programmed and conducted to a tight schedule for maximum efficiency. If you are late your test may be cancelled and you are likely to lose your fee and have to re-apply.

It is your responsibility to make sure you are there in time for the test to start.

If your test is cancelled for this reason or for circumstances such as examiner illness or bad weather, the cancelled appointment won't count as one of the three attempts allowed within the two-year period.

How to apply

Complete the application on the back of the letter informing you of your written test result and send it with the fee to DSA headquarters. If you have lost the letter, contact your local SE ADI or write to DSA headquarters.

Unless you state otherwise, appointments are usually offered within five weeks of application. Waiting times vary from office to office. If you need to arrange a test at the earliest opportunity, it is a good idea to nominate a second choice of office. Your first choice may have a longer waiting time.

However, you can apply for a short notice test which may become available as a result of a sudden cancellation.

You will receive a letter of appointment confirming the date, time and office and you will normally be given at least three weeks notice of this date.

Test of Instructional Ability

Surname and initials (in CAPITALS)

Partridge, W. J.

Address

20, Oaklands, Park Valley,
Llanelli   Postcode **SA14 8OD**

Telephone number including daytime number.

01554 774317

● I apply for admission to the test of instructional ability which forms part of the qualifying examination for the Register of Approved Driving Instructors.

● I confirm that I have read and understand the conditions that apply to the qualifying period (which are given overleaf). This application is for my (please ✓ appropriate box)

1st ☑   2nd ☐   Final ☐ attempt.

Centre at which I wish to be tested

1st choice **Swansea**   2nd choice

Dates on which I will **not** be able to take the test

From: To:

From: To:

From: To:

I enclose the required fee of £ **62 - 00**

Cheque PO/No

Signed

W. J. Partridge

Date
12 . 6 . 97

Area	Centres where tests may be taken	Area	Centres where tests may be taken
London and South East	Barnet Brentwood Canterbury Dartford Eastbourne Guildford Hayes Redhill Sevenoaks Surbiton Wealdstone	Northern	Ellesmere Port Leeds Liverpool (Crosby) Newcastle upon Tyne Preston Rochdale Sale Sheffield Thornaby Wigan
Midlands and Eastern	Birmingham (S. Yardley) Cambridge Colchester Derby Leamington Spa Leicester Lincoln Luton Northampton Norwich Wolverhampton Worcester	Scotland	Aberdeen Edinburgh Glasgow Inverness
Wales and Western	Bristol Cardiff (Barry) Plymouth Southampton Swansea Taunton		

Note: Some centres may be temporarily unavailable. It may be necessary to invite candidates to a nearby alternative centre.

DRIVING
STANDARDS
AGENCY

'Safe driving for life'

Stanley House
56, Talbot Street
NOTTINGHAM
NG1 5GU

Personal Ref No224923
Our Reference OMA28
Our Tel No 0115 901 2608
Date08/12/2000

Dear Mrs
Thank you for your fee for the Driving Ability Test.
Please bring this invitation with you when you come for your test on

DATE :18/12/2000   TIME: 9:15   PLACE: DRIVING STANDARDS AGENCY
MINT HOUSE
6 STANLEY PARK ROAD
WALLINGTON
SURREY

EXAMINER: AN EXAMINER

+++   FIRST ATTEMPT ++++ FIRST ATTEMPT ++++ FIRST ATTEMPT +++++ FIRST ATTEMPT ++++

In case of bad weather please 'phone 01816471097 at least 30 minutes before the test.

1

2

3 SHORT NOTICE

If you cannot attend then complete the section below titled CANCELLATION and return this letter to the address at the top of the page. You should also telephone this office, on the number at the top of the page, before the required 10 days as we cannot be responsible for lost or late mail.

If you do decide to cancel please take note of the 10 day rule.

THE VEHICLE
You must provide a suitable saloon or estate motor car in proper condition, with seat belt in working order, and capable of the normal performance of a vehicle of its type. It should have a manual transmission, right-hand drive, a readily adjustable driving seat, and a seat for a forward facing passenger. If the vehicle does not meet these requirements, the test will not proceed.

INSURANCE
The Department cannot accept responsibility for risks not covered by insurance, including the loss of any No Claims Bonus or the cost of repairing minor damage.

DO NOT DETACH

Yours sincerely

CANCELLATION
THE LAST DAY FOR CANCELLING THIS TEST WITHOUT LOSS OF FEE IS
Only in exceptional circumstances where less than 10 working days notice is given from day of receipt, day of test, weekends and public holidays excluded, will we refund your fee or offer a free re-test.

Please tick as appropriate
I wish to cancel this appointment .. Please refund my fee
Please arrange a new appointment for me......As soon as possible.................Not before.................. (please give date)
Signed

Personal Ref. No.

DETR
ENVIRONMENT
TRANSPORT
REGIONS

An executive agency of the
Department of the Environment,
Transport and the Regions

Providing a suitable vehicle for the test

The vehicle you provide for the test must be a saloon or estate car which is

- fitted with manual transmission (or automatic transmission only if you are the holder of an Emergency Control Certificate (ECC))

- roadworthy and meets all the legal requirements

- fitted with a rigid roof with or without a sun roof (Motor Cars (Driving Instruction) Regulations 1989)

- right hand drive steering (steering wheel fitted on its off-side)

- fitted with a readily-adjustable driver's seat and a forward facing passenger seat

- fitted with seat belts in good working order

- capable of normal performance for a car of its type

- not displaying L plates (D plates in Wales) or giving the impression that it is being driven by a learner driver.

- not going to run out of fuel during the test.

You can use your own car or one you have borrowed, providing it meets all of the above requirements.

The formation and duration of the test

The test will last about one hour and is conducted in two parts

- the eyesight test

- the driving technique test.

You should also allow additional time at the end of the test for the examiner to give you a verbal de-brief and complete the necessary documentation

The eyesight test

You must be able to read, in good daylight, a number plate

- at a distance of 27.5 metres (90 feet)
- with letters and numbers 79.4 mm ($3^1/8$ inches) high.

This can be with or without the aid of glasses or contact lenses.

After the initial greeting, the examiner will

- ask to see your letter of appointment
- request that you read, sign and date a declaration stating the car you are using is properly insured
- ask you to indicate below the declaration whether or not you are exempt from having to wear a seat belt.

The examiner will then invite you to lead the way out and ask you to

- point out the car you have brought for the test
- read the number plate of another vehicle which will be slightly further than the minimum regulation distance.

If you

- read the number correctly you will move on to the test of driving technique
- cannot read the number correctly, the examiner will measure the exact minimum regulation distance from a different vehicle using a tape.

If you cannot read the number correctly at this attempt, the eyesight test will be recorded as a fail and the test of driving technique will not be conducted.

The examiner will give you a copy of the test report.

If you fail the eyesight test, this will count as one of the three attempts you are allowed to pass the Part Two examination.

About the test of your driving technique

Following the eyesight test and once you have got into the car, the examiner will explain that during the test of your driving technique

- you should continue ahead unless the traffic signs or road markings inform you differently

- you will be asked in good time to turn left or right

- the test will include all of the set manoeuvres – including the emergency stop, moving away at an angle and, if practicable, up-hill and down-hill starts

- if you don't understand any of the instructions, don't be afraid to ask – they will be repeated or clarified

- you should drive as you normally do – but remember, a high standard of competence is expected.

Persons who may accompany you during the test

Your trainer may be present during the test. This is up to you. Inform the examiner, who will then advise your trainer to sit in the back and take no part in the conduct of the test. Examiners are often supervised by a senior officer who may also sit in on the test. Don't worry about this; the senior officer is there to ensure that the examiner is conducting and assessing tests to the correct standard and in a uniform manner. The senior officer will not take any part in the conduct of the test.

The test routes

The routes will cover varying road and traffic conditions, and where possible, will include

- rural areas

- urban areas and town centres

- dual carriageways

- motorways.

Make sure your vehicle control, judgement and forward planning are developed to a very high standard. Don't settle for second best – the examiner won't.

If you think or know you have made a mistake during the test, try not to let it worry you.

Think about what you are doing, not what you have done.

How your driving is assessed and marked

Faults are recorded on the test report form – ADI 25.

If your action or reaction to a situation is incorrect it will be assessed and marked accordingly.

DRIVING
STANDARDS
AGENCY

Tests 1 and 2
Eyesight and Driving Technique

Declaration
- I declare that my use of the test vehicle for the purpose of the test is covered by a valid policy of insurance which satisfies the requirement of the relevant legislation
- I do/do not have to wear seat belts under the Motor Vehicles (Wearing of Seat Belts) Regulations 1982.

Signed

Date

Centre

Date

Make & model

Reg Mark

Dual Controls   Fitted   Not Fitted

Candidate's Name

Ref. No

Eyesight test

1. Compliance with the requirements of the eyesight test

Control

2. Take proper precautions before starting the engine

3. Make proper use of:-

accelerator   clutch   gears

footbrake   handbrake   steering

4. Move away:-   safely   under control

5. Stop vehicle in an emergency promptly and under control

6. Reverse left into a limited opening:-
under control   with proper observation   reasonably accurately

7. Reverse right into a limited opening:-
under control   with proper observation   reasonably accurately

8. Reverse parking:-
under control   with proper observation   reasonably accurately

9. Turn in the road:-
under control   with proper observation   reasonably accurately

Road Procedure

10. Make effective use of mirror(s) well before:-

Signalling   changing direction   overtaking

slowing down / stopping

11. Give signals by direction indicators/arm:-
where necessary   correctly   properly timed

Road Procedure (cont)

12. Take prompt and appropriate action on all:-

traffic signs   road markings   traffic lights

signals by traffic controllers   other road users

13. Exercise proper care in the use of speed

14. Make progress by driving at a speed appropriate to the road and traffic conditions avoiding undue hesitancy

15. Keep a safe distance behind vehicles

16. Act properly at road junctions with regard to:-

speed on approach   observation

approaching traffic   position before turning right

position before turning left   right corner cutting

17. Deal with other vehicles safely when:-

overtaking   meeting   crossing their path

18. Position the vehicle correctly:-
during normal driving   exercise lane discipline

19. Allow adequate clearance to stationary vehicles and obstructions

20. Take appropriate action at pedestrian crossings

21. Select a safe position for normal stops

22. Show awareness and anticipation of the actions of:-

pedestrians   cyclists   drivers

23. Use of ancillary controls

Examiner took action: verbal   physical

Test terminated at request of candidate

Supervising Examiner:

Oral debrief   *Offered   *Yes   *No   *Given   *Yes   *No   * Delete as applicable

ADI 25 (Rev 2/98)

Last Printed Feb '98

The assessment and recording of faults comes under three categories depending on how serious they are.

Faults of an insignificant nature are not recorded on the test report.

The marks used to record faults are the same as those used for the L test, but the assessment is of a much higher standard and at a more advanced level.

Faults are marked on the ADI 25 in the following way

- a driving fault   /
- a serious or potentially dangerous driving fault   **X**
- a dangerous driving fault involving actual danger   **D**

Faults of a different nature may occur but are assessed and recorded under the same box headings. For example, if you have a habit of looking down at the gear lever whilst on the move, this will be recorded as a driving fault under the box heading

   Make proper use of: Gears

Likewise, a mis-selection of gears would also be recorded under the box heading

   Make proper use of: Gears

Driving faults

A driving error is assessed and, if considered significant, recorded as a driving fault when

- a mistake in driving technique

or

- an incorrect reaction to a situation

occurs, providing, at that time, the error did not cause potential danger to either

- passengers
- the driver
- any other road users
- buildings and/or property.

It is recorded on the test report by means of an oblique stroke / on the left side of the appropriate box.

A subsequent fault of a different nature (but marked under the same box heading) or a repeat of the same fault is recorded by means of a second oblique stroke / to the right of the first.

Further repetition of driving faults which fall within the same category will not be recorded with a third or subsequent oblique stroke.

However, persistent repetition of the same driving fault or faults, showing a pattern of weakness in driving technique will be assessed and may be recorded as serious.

Serious faults

These are driving faults which involve potentially dangerous situations to either

- passengers
- the driver
- any other road users
- buildings and/or property

or display an unacceptable pattern of weakness in driving technique in one or more aspects of a persons driving will be recorded as serious.

They are recorded by means of a single cross **X** in the centre of the appropriate box against the item to which they refer.

However, if two or more serious faults occur under the same box heading, no further **X** markings will be recorded in that box. That is, an **X** marking in any box is only recorded once.

For example, if two or more serious faults for not moving off safely occurred during the test, only one **X** mark would be recorded in the box headed

Move away safely

Dangerous faults

Dangerous faults are those which involve actual danger to any or all of the following.

- passengers
- the driver
- any other road users
- buildings and/or property

They are recorded by a capital **D** marked on the right of the box.

If two or more dangerous faults occur under the same box heading, no further **D** markings will be recorded in that box. That is, a **D** marking in any box is only recorded once.

Should a person's driving be of very poor quality, the examiner may consider terminating the test in the interest of public safety.

If this happens, an explanation will be offered along with a copy of the test report. The examiner will then return to the test centre alone or with the senior officer on foot.

How the overall assessment is made

You are allowed a maximum of six driving faults (/) throughout the te[st]

Tests 1 and 2
Eyesight and Driving Technique

DRIVING STANDARDS AGENCY

Declaration
- I declare that my use of the test vehicle for the purpose of the test is covered by a valid policy of insurance which satisfies the requirement of the relevant legislation
- I do/do not have to wear seat belts under the Motor Vehicles (Wearing of Seat Belts) Regulations 1982.

Signed

Date

Centre

Date

Make & model

Reg Mark

Dual Controls   Fitted   Not Fitted

Candidate's Name

Ref. No

Eyesight test

1. Compliance with the requirements of the eyesight test

Control

2. Take proper precautions before starting the engine

3. Make proper use of:-

accelerator   clutch   gears

footbrake   handbrake   steering

4. Move away:-   safely   under control /

5. Stop vehicle in an emergency promptly and under control

6. Reverse left into a limited opening:-
under control   with proper observation /   reasonably accurately

7. Reverse right into a limited opening:-
under control   with proper observation /   reasonably accurately

8. Reverse parking:-
under control   with proper observation   reasonably accurately

9. Turn in the road:
under control   with proper observation   reasonably accurately

Road Procedure

10. Make effective use of mirror(s) well before:-

Signalling //   changing direction   overtaking

slowing down / stopping

11. Give signals by direction indicators/arm:-
where necessary   correctly   properly timed

Road Procedure (cont)

12. Take prompt and appropriate action on all:-
traffic signs   road markings   traffic lights

signals by traffic controllers   other road users

13. Exercise proper care in the use of speed

14. Make progress by driving at a speed appropriate to the road and traffic conditions avoiding undue hesitancy

15. Keep a safe distance behind vehicles

16. Act properly at road junctions with regard to:-
speed on approach   observation /
approaching traffic   position before turning right
position before turning left   right corner cutting

17. Deal with other vehicles safely when:-
overtaking   meeting   crossing their path

18. Position the vehicle correctly:-
during normal driving   exercise lane discipline

19. Allow adequate clearance to stationary vehicles and obstructions

20. Take appropriate action at pedestrian crossings

21. Select a safe position for normal stops

22. Show awareness and anticipation of the actions of:-
pedestrians   cyclists   drivers

23. Use of ancillary controls

Examiner took action: verbal   physical

Test terminated at request of candidate

Supervising Examiner:

	*Offered		*Given		* Delete an a
Oral debrief	* Yes	* No	* Yes	* No	

ADI 25 (Rev

Last Printed Feb '98

If seven or more are recorded this will
result in failure.

Tests 1 and 2
Eyesight and Driving Technique

DRIVING
STANDARDS
AGENCY

Declaration
- I declare that my use of the test vehicle for the purpose of the test is covered by a valid policy of insurance which satisfies the requirement of the relevant legislation
- I do/do not have to wear seat belts under the Motor Vehicles (Wearing of Seat Belts) Regulations 1982.

Signed

Date

Centre

Date

Make & model

Reg Mark

Dual Controls   Fitted   Not Fitted

Candidate's Name

Ref. No

Eyesight test

1. Compliance with the requirements of the eyesight test

Control

2. Take proper precautions before starting the engine

3. Make proper use of:-

accelerator   clutch   gears

footbrake   handbrake   steering

4. Move away:-   safely   under control

5. Stop vehicle in an emergency promptly and under control

6. Reverse left into a limited opening:-
under control   with proper observation /   reasonably accurately

7. Reverse right into a limited opening:-
under control   with proper observation   reasonably accurately

8. Reverse parking:-
under control   with proper observation   reasonably accurately

9. Turn in the road:
under control /   with proper observation   reasonably accurately

Road Procedure

10. Make effective use of mirror(s) well before:-
Signalling //   changing direction   overtaking //

slowing down / stopping

11. Give signals by direction indicators/arm:-
where necessary   correctly   properly timed

Road Procedure (cont)

12. Take prompt and appropriate action on all:-
traffic signs   road markings   traffic lights
signals by traffic controllers   other road users

13. Exercise proper care in the use of speed

14. Make progress by driving at a speed appropriate to the road and traffic conditions avoiding undue hesitancy   /

15. Keep a safe distance behind vehicles   /

16. Act properly at road junctions with regard to:-
speed on approach   observation
approaching traffic   position before turning right
position before turning left   right corner cutting

17. Deal with other vehicles safely when:-
overtaking   meeting   crossing their path

18. Position the vehicle correctly:-
during normal driving   exercise lane discipline

19. Allow adequate clearance to stationary vehicles and obstructions

20. Take appropriate action at pedestrian crossings

21. Select a safe position for normal stops

22. Show awareness and anticipation of the actions of:-
pedestrians   cyclists   drivers

23. Use of ancillary controls

Examiner took action: verbal   physical

Test terminated at request of candidate

Supervising Examiner:

Oral debrief	*Offered		*Given		* Delete as applicable
	* Yes	* No	* Yes	* No	

ADI 25 (Rev 2/98)

Last Printed Feb'98

One or more **X** or **D** markings recorded on the ADI 25 will also result in failure to pass.

At the end of the test the examiner will offer a full de-brief about the drive.

Tests 1 and 2
Eyesight and Driving Technique

DRIVING STANDARDS AGENCY

Declaration
- I declare that my use of the test vehicle for the purpose of the test is covered by a valid policy of insurance which satisfies the requirement of the relevant legislation
- I do/do not have to wear seat belts under the Motor Vehicles (Wearing of Seat Belts) Regulations 1982.

Signed

Date

Centre

Date

Make & model

Reg Mark

Dual Controls   Fitted [ ]   Not Fitted [ ]

Candidate's Name

Ref. No

Eyesight test

1. Compliance with the requirements of the eyesight test [ ]

Control

2. Take proper precautions before starting the engine [ ]

3. Make proper use of:-

| accelerator [ ] | clutch [ ] | gears [ ] |
| footbrake [ ] | handbrake [ ] | steering [ ] |

4. Move away:-   safely [ ]   under control [ ]

5. Stop vehicle in an emergency promptly and under control [ ]

6. Reverse left into a limited opening:-
   under control [ ]   with proper observation [ ]   reasonably accurately [ ]

7. Reverse right into a limited opening:-
   under control [ ]   with proper observation [ ]   reasonably accurately [ ]

8. Reverse parking:-
   under control [ ]   with proper observation [ ]   reasonably accurately [ ]

9. Turn in the road:
   under control [ ]   with proper observation [ ]   reasonably accurately [ ]

Road Procedure

10. Make effective use of mirror(s) well before:-
   Signalling [/]   changing direction [ ]   overtaking [**X**]
   slowing down / stopping [ ]

11. Give signals by direction indicators/arm:-
   where necessary [ ]   correctly [ ]   properly timed [ ]

Road Procedure (cont)

12. Take prompt and appropriate action on all:-
   traffic signs [ ]   road markings [ ]   traffic lights [ ]
   signals by traffic controllers [ ]   other road users [ ]

13. Exercise proper care in the use of speed [ ]

14. Make progress by driving at a speed appropriate to the road and traffic conditions avoiding undue hesitancy [/]

15. Keep a safe distance behind vehicles [ ]

16. Act properly at road junctions with regard to:-
   speed on approach [ ]   observation [ ]
   traffic [ ]   position before turning right [ ]
   position before turning left [ ]   right corner cutting [ ]

17. Deal with other vehicles safely when:-
   overtaking [ ]   meeting [ ]   crossing their path [ ]

18. Position the vehicle correctly:-
   during normal driving [ ]   exercise lane discipline [ ]

19. Allow adequate clearance to stationary vehicles and obstructions [ ]

20. Take appropriate action at pedestrian crossings [ ]

21. Select a safe position for normal stops [ ]

22. Show awareness and anticipation of the actions of:-
   pedestrians [ ]   cyclists [ ]   drivers [ ]

23. Use of ancillary controls [ ]

Examiner took action: verbal [ ]   physical [ ]

Test terminated at request of candidate [ ]

Supervising Examiner:

| Oral debrief | *Offered | | *Given | | * Delete as applicable |
| | * Yes | * No | * Yes | * No | |

ADI 25 (Rev 2/98)

Last Printed Feb'98

This would include all repeated **X** or
D faults.

Report of Approved Driving Instructors

Tests 1 and 2
Eyesight and Driving Technique

DRIVING
STANDARDS
AGENCY

Centre	
Date	
Make & model	
Reg Mark	

Dual Controls   Fitted   Not Fitted

Candidate's
Name

Ref. No

Declaration

- I declare that my use of the test vehicle for the purpose of the test is covered by a valid policy of insurance which satisfies the requirement of the relevant legislation
- I do/do not have to wear seat belts under the Motor Vehicles (Wearing of Seat Belts) Regulations 1982.

Signed

Date

Eyesight test

1. Compliance with the requirements of the eyesight test

Control

2. Take proper precautions before starting the engine

3. Make proper use of:-

accelerator   clutch   gears

footbrake   handbrake   steering

4. Move away:-   safely   under control

5. Stop vehicle in an emergency promptly and under control

6. Reverse left into a limited opening:-
   under control   **X** with proper observation   reasonably accurately

7. Reverse right into a limited opening:-
   under control   with proper observation   reasonably accurately

8. Reverse parking:-
   under control   with proper observation   reasonably accurately

9. Turn in the road:-
   under control   with proper observation   reasonably accurately

Road Procedure

10. Make effective use of mirror(s) well before:-

Signalling   changing direction   overtaking

slowing down / stopping

11. Give signals by direction indicators/arm:-
where necessary   correctly   properly timed

Road Procedure (cont)

12. Take prompt and appropriate action on all:-
traffic signs   road markings   traffic lights   other road users

signals by traffic controllers

13. Exercise proper care in the use of speed

14. Make progress by driving at a speed appropriate to the road and traffic conditions avoiding undue hesitancy

15. Keep a safe distance behind vehicles

16. Act properly at road junctions with regard to:-
speed on approach   observation **D**
approaching traffic   position before turning right
position before turning left   right corner cutting

17. Deal with other vehicles safely when:-
overtaking   meeting   crossing their path

18. Position the vehicle correctly:-
during normal driving   exercise lane discipline

19. Allow adequate clearance to stationary vehicles and obstructions

20. Take appropriate action at pedestrian crossings

21. Select a safe position for normal stops

22. Show awareness and anticipation of the actions of:-
pedestrians   cyclists   drivers

23. Use of ancillary controls

Examiner took action: verbal   physical

Test terminated at request of candidate

Supervising Examiner

Oral debrief	*Offered		*Given		* Delete as applicable
	* Yes	* No	* Yes	* No	

ADI 25 (Rev 2/98)

Last Printed Feb '98

Not all of the boxes are marked in the same way

Some of the boxes are only marked with one of the assessment marks.

Box number 1

Compliance with the requirements of the eyesight test

This box would only be marked with an **X** in the event of failure to read a number plate at the regulation distance.

Eyesight test
1. Compliance with the requirements of the eyesight test

Box number 5

Stop the vehicle in an emergency

- promptly
- under control.

5. Stop vehicle in an emergency promptly and under control

Box number 6

Reverse left into a limited opening

- under control
- with proper observation
- reasonably accurately.

6. Reverse left into a limited opening:-
under control   with proper observation   reasonably accurately

Box number 7

Reverse right into a limited opening

- under control
- with proper observation
- reasonably accurately.

7. Reverse right into a limited opening:-
under control   with proper observation   reasonably accurately

Box number 8
Reverse parking

- under control
- with proper observation
- reasonably accurately.

8. Reverse parking:-		
under control	with proper observation	reasonably accurately

Box number 9
Turn in the road

- under control
- with proper observation
- reasonably accurately.

9. Turn in the road:		
under control	with proper observation	reasonably accurately

Each of these boxes on the ADI 25 numbered 1 and 5 to 9 (inclusive) are assessed and marked (if appropriate) after the exercise has been completed.

As these exercises 5 to 9 are only conducted once, the examiner need only make one overall assessment on each of the sub-categories

- under control
- with proper observation
- reasonably accurately.

For example, during the reverse parking exercise a candidate commits a

- driving fault   /

and

- serious fault   X

regarding 'under control';

Eyesight test

Eyesight test		
1. Compliance with the requirements of the eyesight test		

Control

2. Take proper precautions before starting the engine		
3. Make proper use of:-		
accelerator	clutch	gears
footbrake	handbrake	steering
4. Move away:-	safely	under control
5. Stop vehicle in an emergency promptly and under control		
6. Reverse left into a limited opening:-		
under control	with proper observation	reasonably accurately
7. Reverse right into a limited opening:-		
under control	with proper observation	reasonably accurately
8. Reverse parking:-		
under control	with proper observation	reasonably accurately
9. Turn in the road:		
under control	with proper observation	reasonably accurately

also

- a serious fault 'X'

and

- a dangerous fault 'D'

regarding 'with proper observation'.

Only the most severe marks in each of the sub-categories would be recorded on the ADI 25.

Box number 8
Reverse parking

In this example

- only an **X** would be recorded in the box marked 'under control'

and

- only a **D** would be recorded in the box marked 'with proper observation'.

In the bottom right corner of the ADI 25

Examiner took action

would only be marked with an **X** when appropriate.

Any of the other boxes could have the maximum four marks recorded

The result

You will be informed of the result at the end of the test.

If you fail the examiner will offer you a

- debrief on all faults recorded (your trainer can be present)
- copy of the test report (ADI 25)
- letter confirming the result (ADI 10D).

On the back of this letter there is an application form. This can be used to apply to re-sit the Part Two test **provided you have not used up your three attempts.**

You may appeal if you consider your test was not conducted properly in accordance with the regulations.

You can't appeal against the examiner's decision just because you don't agree with it. See Section Seven.

If you pass you will be

- offered a debrief on all driving faults recorded
- invited to have your trainer present during the debrief
- given a copy of the test report (ADI 25)
- offered a trainee licence application form (ADI 3L)
- handed a letter confirming the result (ADI 11).

On the back of this letter there is an application form for the Part Three test. It should only be completed and sent with the correct fee to DSA headquarters **when you are fully prepared for the next stage.**

When you have passed the Part Two test you are entitled to apply for a trainee licence. This is explained in more detail in the next section.

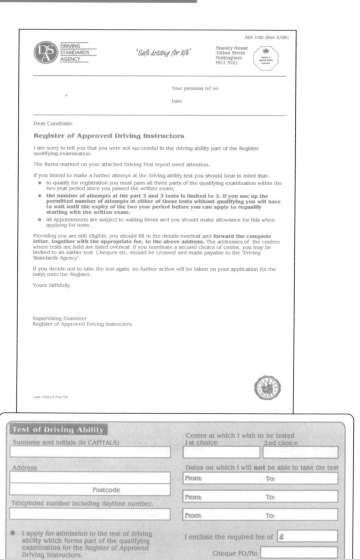

ADI 10D (Rev 2/98)

DRIVING
STANDARDS
AGENCY

"Safe driving for life"

Stanley House
Talbot Street
Nottingham
NG1 5GU.

Your personal ref no

Date

Dear Candidate

Register of Approved Driving Instructors

I am sorry to tell you that you were not successful in the driving ability part of the Register qualifying examination.

The items marked on your attached Driving Test report need attention.

If you intend to make a further attempt at the driving ability test you should bear in mind that:-

- to qualify for registration you must pass all three parts of the qualifying examination within the two year period since you passed the written exam;
- **the number of attempts at the part 2 and 3 tests is limited to 3. If you use up the permitted number of attempts at either of these tests without qualifying you will have to wait until the expiry of the two year period before you can apply to requalify starting with the written exam;**
- all appointments are subject to waiting times and you should make allowance for this when applying for tests.

Providing you are still eligible, you should fill in the details overleaf and **forward the complete letter, together with the appropriate fee, to the above address.** The addresses of the centres where tests are held are listed overleaf. If you nominate a second choice of centre, you may be invited to an earlier test. Cheques etc. should be crossed and made payable to the 'Driving Standards Agency'.

If you decide not to take the test again, no further action will be taken on your application for the entry onto the Register.

Yours faithfully

Supervising Examiner
Register of Approved Driving Instructors

Last Printed Feb'98

Test of Driving Ability

Surname and initials (in CAPITALS)

Centre at which I wish to be tested
1st choice   2nd choice

Address

Dates on which I will **not** be able to take the test

From: To:

Postcode

From: To:

Telephone number including daytime number.

From: To:

- I apply for admission to the test of driving ability which forms part of the qualifying examination for the Register of Approved Driving Instructors.

I enclose the required fee of £

Cheque PO/No

- I confirm that I have read and understand the conditions that apply to the qualifying period (which are given overleaf). This application is for my

Signed

1st ☐   2nd ☐   Final ☐   attempt.

(please ✓ appropriate box)

Date

ADI 11 (1/96)

DRIVING
STANDARDS
AGENCY

"Safe driving for life"

Stanley House
Talbot Street
Nottingham
NG1 5GU.

Your personal ref no

Date

Dear Candidate

Register of Approved Driving Instructors

I am glad to tell you that you were successful in the driving ability part of the Register qualifying examination. You may now apply to take the final part of the examination, the test of instructional ability, but please bear in mind the following:

- To qualify for registration you must pass all 3 parts of the qualifying examination within the 2 year period since you passed the written exam.
- **You are permitted only 3 attempts at the instructional ability test. If you do not pass within the 2 year period or on your final attempt at this test, whichever is the sooner, you will have to wait until the expiry of the 2 year period before you can apply to requalify, starting with the written exam.**
- All appointments are subject to waiting times and you should make allowances for this when applying for tests.

To apply for the test of instructional ability you should fill in the details overleaf and **forward this complete letter, together with the appropriate fee, to the above address.** The addresses of the centres where tests are held, are listed overleaf. It is essential to nominate a second choice of centre. You may then be invited to an earlier test. Cheques etc should be crossed and made payable to the Driving Standards Agency.

You must provide a car for the test of instructional ability. The Department's requirements regarding the car to be used for this test are the same as for the test of driving ability which you have just taken, except for 2 items. Firstly, there is no need for the car to be free from driving school signs but it must display 'L' plates. Secondly, for the time during which the examiner is driving the car, insurance must be provided to cover the examiner's liability for all third party risks and for his/her liability to any passenger, including any official passenger.

Now that you have passed the first 2 parts of the examination you may apply for a licence to give instruction if you so wish. However, you should first read the booklet ADI 14 which explains the important requirements and conditions which relate to the grant of a licence.

Yours faithfully

Supervising Examiner
Register of Approved Driving Instructors

Test of Instructional Ability

Surname and initials (in CAPITALS)

Centre at which I wish to be tested

1st choice | 2nd choice

Address

Dates on which I will **not** be able to take the test

From: | To:

Postcode

From: | To:

Telephone number including daytime number.

From: | To:

- I apply for admission to the test of instructional ability which forms part of the qualifying examination for the Register of Approved Driving Instructors.

- I confirm that I have read and understand the conditions that apply to the qualifying period (which are given overleaf).

Signed

I enclose the required fee of £

Cheque PO/No

Date

The topics covered

- The trainee licence system
- About the test
- Core competencies
- Instructional techniques
- Instructor characteristics
- The examiner's assessment

The trainee licence system

As with Parts One and Two, quality training and preparation are essential.

A trainee licence gives you the opportunity to receive payment for lessons while gaining practical experience. A training school is allowed a maximum ratio of one trainee for each qualified ADI. This practical experience can help you prepare for the Part Three test.

However, it is possible to pass the Part Three test without having a Trainee Licence. It is for you to decide whether or not it is worth your while. You should discuss this with your trainer.

If you don't have a trainee licence you may instruct friends or relatives, so long as no payment of money or money's worth is involved. It is worth considering that teaching friends and relatives can be quite different from teaching a complete stranger or someone you hardly know.

You must receive training in every one of the following core curriculum subjects.

- Explaining the controls of the car, including the use of dual controls.
- Moving off.
- Making normal stops.
- Using mirrors and giving correct signals.
- Road positioning.
- Approaching and turning corners.
- Dealing with road junctions.
- Explaining how to make an emergency stop.
- Dealing with crossroads.
- Comprehension of traffic signs including road markings and traffic control signals.
- Allowing adequate clearance for other vehicles and other road users.
- Overtaking, meeting and crossing the path of other vehicles and other road users.
- Judgement of speed and making normal progress.
- Dealing with pedestrian crossings.
- Turning to face the opposite direction using forward and reverse gears.
- Reversing into limited openings to the left and right.
- Parking close to the kerb using forward and reverse gears.
- Method, clarity, adequacy and correctness of instruction.
- General manner, patience and tact in dealing with pupils.
- Ability to inspire confidence in pupils.

The conditions under which a trainee licence is issued

Anyone can apply for a trainee licence providing that they

- hold a British or Northern Ireland car driving licence or hold a European Union (EU)/ European Economic Area (EEA) licence.
- have held that licence for a total of four years out of the past six years prior to entering the Register after qualifying. A foreign driving licence, an automatic car driving licence or a provisional licence held after passing the driving test all count towards the four years.
- complete the required minimum 40 hours training in the core subjects.
- have not been disqualified from driving at any time in the four years up to the date of application.
- are a fit and proper person – see Section Six.
- have passed the written part of the qualifying exam and the practical test of driving technique.
- are eligible to take the test of instructional ability.

- are within the two-year qualifying period before the date of your application.

- do not cause the sponsoring driving school to exceed the maximum ratio of one trainee licence holder to one ADI.

How to apply for a trainee licence

You can obtain an application form (ADI 3L) from an ADI SE office or by writing to DSA headquarters. Complete and send it with the licence fee and two passport photos of yourself to DSA headquarters. Apart from very exceptional circumstances you will only be granted one licence.

You should receive a pink Licence of Registration by post, within one week of your application being received at DSA headquarters. It will have affixed to it one of the passport photographs. The licence also records your name, your Personal Reference Number, and the dates of issue and expiry.

The regulations specify that whenever you are charging for driving instruction your trainee licence must be fixed to, and immediately behind, the front windscreen of the car you are teaching in. It should be displayed on the near-side edge of the screen so that the particulars on the back are clearly visible from the outside. The particulars on the front must be clearly visible from the nearside front seat.

The licence is valid for six months. It is granted so that you have the opportunity to gain practical experience in developing your instructional skills. However, it should not be considered as an alternative to registration.

Register of Approved Driving Instructors   ADI 3L (Rev 6/94)

Application for a Trainee Licence

● Please read the Notes sheet   ✍ in CAPITALS   ✓ the boxes

1. Your Details

Title   Mr ☐   Mrs ☐   Miss ☐   Ms ☐

Surname

First name(s)

Home address

Postcode

☎ (inc STD Code)

What is your personal reference No?

What is your Driver No? (shown on your licence)

● Have you ever been issued with a licence to give instruction?

Yes ☐   No ☐

● Have you passed both the written and driving ability parts of the qualifying exams in the last two years?

Yes ☐   No ☐

Please give exact date and centre where you passed the driving ability test, and the name of the examiner (if known).

Date

Centre

Date licence to start (Mondays only) * see below

* We may not be able to alter the start date once the licence is issued.

Please give the name and address of the training school from which you will give instruction.

Postcode

☎ (inc STD Code)

Give the name and ADI number of your trainer

2. Character Details

● Have you been convicted of a non-motoring or motoring offence since the date you applied for registration?

Your Driver Licence details may be checked to verify motoring offence details.

Non-Motoring ☐   Motoring ☐   None ☐

If you have please give details
Offence(s) (use a separate sheet if necessary)

Name of court and date of conviction

Penalty imposed (including any endorsements)

Are court proceedings of any kind pending against you?   Yes ☐   No ☐

If 'yes', please give details
Alleged offence(s) (use separate sheet if necessary)

Name of court (if known)

Date of hearing (if known)

There are two ways you can satisfy the training conditions attached to the licence.

Option 1 – by supervision

At least 20% of the time you spend giving paid instruction must be under the direct supervision of an ADI trainer for the duration of your licence.

A record of this supervision must be kept and submitted to DSA HQ on the expiry of your trainee licence or when you register as a qualified ADI, whichever is the soonest.

Option 2 – by direct training

You must take a further minimum of 20 hours of training on the core subjects within three months of the issue of an ADI trainee licence or by the time you apply for the ADI Part Three test.

At least 25% of this training has to be practical training undertaken in a car, with a maximium instructor ratio of no more than one ADI trainer to two trainee licence holders.

You must keep a record of training you have received. You will be required to produce evidence of this at the end of your three-month period or when you apply for the Part Three test.

If you are unsuccessful at an attempt of the Part Three test you are obliged to undertake a further minimum of 5 hours training under the conditions outlined above. If you fail your third attempt of the Part Three test you have to start the qualifying process again. You must wait until a period of two years has elapsed from the date you passed the written test.

If you sign the form to say that you have had training when in fact you have not, both you and your sponsoring ADI may be committing an offence under section 174 of the Road Traffic Act 1988. Make sure that you get this training – don't sign a blank form.

If you have any difficulty complying with these conditions, for example, if your trainer is not

- giving you the necessary support
- meeting the minimum 40 hours practical training requirements
- accompanying you for at least 20% of the time you are giving paid tuition for the duration of your licence

you should inform either your local SE ADI or DSA headquarters and seek advice at the earliest opportunity.

It's your responsibility to adhere to the conditions attached to your licence.

You must not advertise yourself as a qualified instructor. The Registrar can revoke your licence if any of the conditions under which it was granted are not kept or it was issued by default or gained by fraud.

Licence refunds

Refunds are not given for any period when your licence is not used or for any outstanding time if you pass the instructional ability test before it expires.

What to do if you can't use your licence

If for any reason you are prevented from making full use of your licence and you have to stop giving tuition, return it to DSA headquarters immediately. You won't get any money back, but it may provide grounds for the issue of a second licence.

What to do if your licence is lost or stolen

Report it to the police and advise DSA headquarters.

This test measuring your ability to give effective instruction is generally considered the most difficult of the three qualifying tests and is often referred to as the Part Three test. The object of this test is to assess the value of the instruction you give and your ability to pass on your knowledge to your pupil.

A DSA examiner will sit in the driving seat and role-play the part of a learner driver. This enables a direct assessment to be made without the intervention of a third party.

In this section of the text the word 'pupil' refers to the examiner.

The number of attempts to qualify is limited to three. It is in your interest to ensure you are well prepared.

Waiting times for an instructional test

The average waiting time is five to six weeks. This may vary in some areas due to demand and examiner availability. You can sometimes avoid delays if you state an alternative centre on the application form. It is up to you to decide when you are ready to take the test.

Where the tests are conducted

As with Part Two, the tests are conducted during normal office hours, usually from an SE ADI office. The locations are listed on the application form and in Section Seven. Allow plenty of time for your journey to the office. If you are late your test may be cancelled and you are likely to lose your fee and have to re-apply.

It's your responsibility to make sure you are there in time for the exam to start.

Persons who may accompany you on test

Your trainer may sit in the back, at your request, or you may be accompanied by the examiner's supervising officer. As with the Part Two test the supervisor is present to ensure that a uniform standard of marking and assessment is being adhered to by examiners.

What the test consists of

The test lasts for one hour and is in two parts or phases. Each phase lasts for approximately half an hour. The examiner will ask you to give instruction on one of 12 exercises in each phase and will assess your ability to instruct.

Subjects the test covers

The following is a list of the exercise numbers and the subjects contained in each

Exercise number	Subject(s)
1	Safety precautions on entering the car and explanation of controls.
2	Moving off, making normal stops and use of the mirrors.
3	Reversing.
4	Turning the vehicle round in the road.
5	Parallel parking.
6	Emergency stop and use of the mirrors.
7	Approaching and turning corners.
8	Judgment of speed and general road positioning.
9	Dealing with road junctions.
10	Dealing with crossroads.
11	Meeting, crossing the path of, overtaking other vehicles, allowing adequate clearance for other road users and anticipation.
12	Dealing with pedestrian crossings, giving appropriate signals in a clear and unmistakable manner.

There are ten Pre-Set Test (PST) papers which are numbered as ADI 26/PT 1 to 10.

In the case of re-tests, it is unlikely that you will be given the same PST as on a previous occasion.

To ensure a balance between one phase and the next, the selection of the subjects is not left to the examiner but follows the sequence shown in the following table.

Pre-set test table

Pre-set test number	Phase I Beginner – exercise number	Phase II Partly trained – exercise number	Phase II Trained – exercise number
ADI 26/PT/1	1	-	10
ADI 26/PT/2	2	-	11
ADI 26/PT/3	-	4	7
ADI 26/PT/4	-	3	9
ADI 26/PT/5	-	6	8
ADI 26/PT/6	-	12	5
ADI 26/PT/7	-	7	12
ADI 26/PT/8	-	9	11
ADI 26/PT/9	-	10	12
ADI 26/PT/10	-	11	8

The PST shown overleaf will be used to explain the examiner's assessment later in this section.

Instructional Test - Part III

DRIVING STANDARDS AGENCY

The Examiner has marked each aspect of your performance in columns A and B below. Please see overleaf for explanatory notes.

Candidate's Declaration

I certify that
- the vehicle I have provided for the test is properly insured under the Road Traffic Act 1988 and
- I do/do not have to wear seat belts under the Motor Vehicles (Wearing of Seat Belts) Regulations 1982.

Signed

Date

Centre	DEVONWOOD
Date	30.1. 2000
Make & model	FORD ESCORT
Reg Mark	N512 CTW

Dual Controls   Fitted ☑   Not Fitted

Candidate's Name

Ref. No

Column A

PST No.4 Exercises 3P and 9T

Phase 1-3P Partly trained-Reversing

Left Reverse ☐   Right Reverse ☐

	Not Covered	Unsatisfactory	Satisfactory
Briefing on reversing	☐	☐	☐
Co-ordination of controls	☐	☐	☐
Observation	☐	☐	☐
Accuracy	☐	☐	☐

Phase 2-9T Trained-T Junctions-Emerging

	Not Covered	Unsatisfactory	Satisfactory
Mirror-Signal-Manoeuvre	☐	☐	☐
Speed	☐	☐	☐
Gears	☐	☐	☐
Coasting	☐	☐	☐
Observation	☐	☐	☐
Emerging	☐	☐	☐
Position right	☐	☐	☐
Position left	☐	☐	☐
Pedestrians	☐	☐	☐

The results of your test are:

Phase I Grade ☐   Phase II Grade ☐

Supervising Examiner's name

Location   Section No.

S E Signature

Column B

In this column the top line of boxes refer to Phase I and the bottom line of boxes refer to Phase II

1/2/3 = Unsatisfactory   4/5/6 = Satisfactory

Core Competencies

	1 2 3	4 5 6
Identification of faults	☐☐☐	☐☐☐
Fault analysis	☐☐☐	☐☐☐
Remedial action	☐☐☐	☐☐☐

Instructional Techniques

	1 2 3	4 5 6
Level of instruction	☐☐☐	☐☐☐
Planning	☐☐☐	☐☐☐
Control of lesson	☐☐☐	☐☐☐
Communication	☐☐☐	☐☐☐
Q/A Techniques	☐☐☐	☐☐☐
Feedback/Encouragement	☐☐☐	☐☐☐
Instructor use of controls	☐☐☐	☐☐☐

Instructor Characteristics

	1 2 3	4 5 6
Attitude and Approach to Pupil	☐☐☐	☐☐☐

ADI 26/PT/04 Rev 7/98

FORMS UK plc (CN7361/500)

Instructional Test - Part III

The Examiner has marked each aspect of your performance in columns A and B below. Please see overleaf for explanatory notes.

DRIVING STANDARDS AGENCY

Centre	DEVONWOOD
Date	30.1.2000
Make & model	FORD ESCORT
Reg Mark	N512 CTW

Dual Controls   Fitted ✓   Not Fitted

Candidate's Name

Ref. No

Candidate's Declaration

I certify that
- the vehicle I have provided for the test is properly insured under the Road Traffic Act 1988 and
- I do/do not have to wear seat belts under the Motor Vehicles (Wearing of Seat Belts) Regulations 1982.

Signed

Date

Column A

PST No.1 Exercises 1B and 10T

Phase 1-1B Beginner-Controls

	Not Covered	Unsatisfactory	Satisfactory
Doors			
Seat/Head Restraint			
Seat Belt			
Mirrors			
Accelerator			
Footbrake			
Clutch			
Handbrake			
Gears			
Steering			
Indicators			
Starting			
Precautions before moving off			
Normal stop position			
Normal stop use of MSM			
Normal stop control			

Phase 2-10T Trained-Crossroads

Mirror-Signal-Manoeuvre			
Speed			
Gears			
Coasting			
Observation			
Emerging			
Position right			
Position left			
Pedestrians			
Cross approaching traffic			
Right corner cut			

The results of your test are:

Phase I Grade

Phase II Grade

Supervising Examiner's name

Location

Section No.

S E Signature

Column B

In this column the top line of boxes to Phase I and the bottom line of boxes refer to Phase II

1/2/3 = **Unsatisfactory**   4/5/6 = **Satisfactory**

Core Competencies

	1 2 3	4 5 6
Identification of faults		
Fault analysis		
Remedial action		

Instructional Techniques

	1 2 3	4 5 6
Level of instruction		
Planning		
Control of lesson		
Communication		
Q/A Techniques		
Feedback/Encouragement		
Instructor use of controls		

Instructor Characteristics

	1 2 3	4 5 6
Attitude and Approach to Pupil		

ADI 26/PT/01 Rev 7/98

FORMS UK plc FC917655I490

Instructional Test - Part III

DRIVING STANDARDS AGENCY

The Examiner has marked each aspect of your performance in columns A and B below. Please see overleaf for explanatory notes.

Register of Approved Driving Instructors (ADI)

Candidate's Declaration

I certify that
- the vehicle I have provided for the test is properly insured under the Road Traffic Act 1988 and
- I do/do not have to wear seat belts under the Motor Vehicles (Wearing of Seat Belts) Regulations 1982.

Signed

Date

Centre	DEVONWOOD
Date	30.1.2000
Make & model	FORD ESCORT
Reg Mark	N512 CTW
Dual Controls	Fitted ✓ Not Fitted
Candidate's Name	
Ref. No	

Column A

PST No.2 Exercises 2B and 11T

Phase 1-2B Beginner-Moving off / stopping

	Not Covered	Unsatisfactory	Satisfactory
Briefing on moving off/stopping			
Mirrors vision and use			
Mirrors, direction, overtaking and stopping			
Mirror signal manoeuvre			
Precautions before moving off			
Co-ordination of controls			
Normal stop position			
Normal stop control			

Phase 2-11T Trained-Meet, cross and overtake other traffic allowing adequate clearance for other road users and anticipation

Mirror-Signal-Manoeuvre			
Meet approaching traffic			
Cross approaching traffic			
Overtake other traffic			
Keep a safe distance			
Shaving other vehicles			
Anticipation of pedestrians			
Anticipation of cyclists			
Anticipation of drivers			

The results of your test are:

Phase I Grade		Phase II Grade	

Supervising Examiner's name

Location   Section No.

S E Signature

Column B

In this column the top line of boxes to Phase I and the bottom line of boxes refer to Phase II

1/2/3 = Unsatisfactory   4/5/6 = Satisfactory

Core Competencies

	1 2 3	4 5 6
Identification of faults		
Fault analysis		
Remedial action		

Instructional Techniques

	1 2 3	4 5 6
Level of instruction		
Planning		
Control of lesson		
Communication		
Q/A Techniques		
Feedback/Encouragement		
Instructor use of controls		

Instructor Characteristics

	1 2 3	4 5 6
Attitude and Approach to Pupil		

ADI 26/PT/02 Rev 7/98

FORMS UK plc

DRIVING STANDARDS AGENCY

Instructional Test - Part III

The Examiner has marked each aspect of your performance in columns A and B below. Please see overleaf for explanatory notes.

Candidate's Declaration

I certify that
- the vehicle I have provided for the test is properly insured under the Road Traffic Act 1988 and
- I do/do not have to wear seat belts under the Motor Vehicles (Wearing of Seat Belts) Regulations 1982.

Signed

Date

Centre	DEVONWOOD
Date	30.1. 2000
Make & model	FORD ESCORT
Reg Mark	N512 CTW

Dual Controls   Fitted ☑   Not Fitted

Candidate's Name

Ref. No

Column A

PST No.3 Exercises 4P and 7T

Phase 1-4P Partly trained-Turn in the road

	Not Covered	Unsatisfactory	Satisfactory
Briefing on turn in the road			
Co-ordination of controls			
Observation			
Accuracy			

Phase 2-7T Trained-Approaching junctions to turn either right or left

	Not Covered	Unsatisfactory	Satisfactory
Mirrors			
Signal			
Brakes			
Gears			
Coasting			
Too fast on approach			
Too slow on approach			
Position			
Pedestrians			
Cross approaching traffic			
Right corner cut			

The results of your test are:

Phase I Grade   Phase II Grade

Supervising Examiner's name

Location   Section No.

S E Signature

Column B

In this column the top line of boxes to Phase I and the bottom line of boxes refer to Phase II

1/2/3 = Unsatisfactory   4/5/6 = Satisfactory

Core Competencies   1 2 3   4 5 6

	1	2	3	4	5	6
Identification of faults						
Fault analysis						
Remedial action						

Instructional Techniques   1 2 3   4 5 6

	1	2	3	4	5	6
Level of instruction						
Planning						
Control of lesson						
Communication						
Q/A Techniques						
Feedback/Encouragement						
Instructor use of controls						

Instructor Characteristics   1 2 3   4 5 6

	1	2	3	4	5	6
Attitude and Approach to Pupil						

ADI 26/PT/03 Rev 7/98

FORVIS UK plc 0115 967 5700

Instructional Test - Part III

The Examiner has marked each aspect of your performance in columns A and B below. Please see overleaf for explanatory notes.

DRIVING STANDARDS AGENCY

Candidate's Declaration

I certify that
- the vehicle I have provided for the test is properly insured under the Road Traffic Act 1988 and
- I do/do not have to wear seat belts under the Motor Vehicles (Wearing of Seat Belts) Regulations 1982.

Signed

Date

Centre **DEVONWOOD**

Date **30.1. 2000**

Make & model **FORD ESCORT**

Reg Mark **N512 CTW**

Dual Controls   Fitted ☑   Not Fitted

Candidate's Name

Ref. No

Column A

PST No.4 Exercises 3P and 9T

Phase 1-3P Partly trained-Reversing

Left Reverse   Right Reverse

	Not Covered	Unsatisfactory	Satisfactory
Briefing on reversing			
Co-ordination of controls			
Observation			
Accuracy			

Phase 2-9T Trained-T Junctions-Emerging

	Not Covered	Unsatisfactory	Satisfactory
Mirror-Signal-Manoeuvre			
Speed			
Gears			
Coasting			
Observation			
Emerging			
Position right			
Position left			
Pedestrians			

The results of your test are:

Phase I Grade   Phase II Grade

Supervising Examiner's name

Location   Section No.

S E Signature

Column B

In this column the top line of boxes to Phase I and the bottom line of boxes refer to Phase II

1/2/3 = Unsatisfactory   4/5/6 = Satisfactory

Core Competencies   1 2 3   4 5 6

- Identification of faults
- Fault analysis
- Remedial action

Instructional Techniques   1 2 3   4 5 6

- Level of instruction
- Planning
- Control of lesson
- Communication
- Q/A Techniques
- Feedback/Encouragement
- Instructor use of controls

Instructor Characteristics   1 2 3   4 5 6

- Attitude and Approach to Pupil

ADI 26/PT/04 Rev 7/98

FORMS UK plc FONT/0572R0

Instructional Test - Part III

DRIVING STANDARDS AGENCY

The Examiner has marked each aspect of your performance in columns A and B below. Please see overleaf for explanatory notes.

Register of Approved Driving Instructors (GB)

Candidate's Declaration

I certify that
- the vehicle I have provided for the test is properly insured under the Road Traffic Act 1988 and
- I do/do not have to wear seat belts under the Motor Vehicles (Wearing of Seat Belts) Regulations 1982.

Signed

Date

Centre	DEVONWOOD
Date	30.1. 2000
Make & model	FORD ESCORT
Reg Mark	N512 CTW

Dual Controls   Fitted ✓   Not Fitted

Candidate's Name

Ref. No

Column A

PST No.5 Exercises 6P and 8T

Phase 1-6P Partly trained-Emergency stop/Mirrors

	Not Covered	Unsatisfactory	Satisfactory
Briefing on emergency stop/mirrors			
Quick reaction			
Use of footbrake/clutch			
Skidding			
Mirrors vision and use			
Mirrors, direction, overtaking and stopping			
Mirror-signal-manoeuvre			

Phase 2-8T Trained-Progress / Hesitancy - Normal position

	Not Covered	Unsatisfactory	Satisfactory
Progress to fast			
Progress too slow			
Hesitancy			
Normal position too wide from the left			
Normal position too close to the left			

The results of your test are:

Phase I Grade   Phase II Grade

Supervising Examiner's name

Location   Section No.

S E Signature

Column B

In this column the top line of boxes to Phase I and the bottom line of boxes refer to Phase II

1/2/3 = Unsatisfactory   4/5/6 = Satisfactory

Core Competencies

	1 2 3	4 5 6
Identification of faults		
Fault analysis		
Remedial action		

Instructional Techniques

	1 2 3	4 5 6
Level of instruction		
Planning		
Control of lesson		
Communication		
Q/A Techniques		
Feedback/Encouragement		
Instructor use of controls		

Instructor Characteristics

	1 2 3	4 5 6
Attitude and Approach to Pupil		

ADI 26/PT/05 Rev 7/98

FORMS UK plc FCN170370000

Instructional Test - Part III

The Examiner has marked each aspect of your performance in columns A and B below. Please see overleaf for explanatory notes.

DRIVING STANDARDS AGENCY

Candidate's Declaration

I certify that
- the vehicle I have provided for the test is properly insured under the Road Traffic Act 1988 and
- I do/do not have to wear seat belts under the Motor Vehicles (Wearing of Seat Belts) Regulations 1982.

Signed

Date

Centre	DEVONWOOD
Date	30.1.2000
Make & model	FORD ESCORT
Reg Mark	N512 CTW

Dual Controls   Fitted ☑   Not Fitted

Candidate's Name

Ref. No

Column A

PST No.6 Exercises 12P and 5T

Phase 1-12P Partly trained-Pedestrian crossings and the use of signals

	Not Covered	Unsatisfactory	Satisfactory
Briefing on pedestrian crossings/signals			
Mirror-signal-manoeuvre			
Speed on approach			
Stop when necessary			
Overtaking on approach			
Inviting pedestrains to cross			
Signals by indicator			
Signals by arm			
Signals - timing			
Unneccessary signals			

Phase 2-5T Trained-Reverse parking

	Not Covered	Unsatisfactory	Satisfactory
Briefing on reverse parking			
Co-ordination of controls			
Observation			
Accuracy			

The results of your test are:

Phase I Grade   Phase II Grade

Supervising Examiner's name

Location   Section No.

S E Signature

Column B

In this column the top line of boxes to Phase 1 and the bottom line of boxes refer to Phase II

1/2/3 = Unsatisfactory   4/5/6 = Satisfactory

Core Competencies   1 2 3   4 5 6

	1 2 3	4 5 6
Identification of faults		
Fault analysis		
Remedial action		

Instructional Techniques   1 2 3   4 5 6

	1 2 3	4 5 6
Level of instruction		
Planning		
Control of lesson		
Communication		
Q/A Techniques		
Feedback/Encouragement		
Instructor use of controls		

Instructor Characteristics   1 2 3   4 5 6

	1 2 3	4 5 6
Attitude and Approach to Pupil		

ADI 26/PT/06 Rev 7/98

FORMS UK plc

Instructional Test - Part III

The Examiner has marked each aspect of your performance in columns A and B below. Please see overleaf for explanatory notes.

DRIVING STANDARDS AGENCY

Candidate's Declaration

I certify that
- the vehicle I have provided for the test is properly insured under the Road Traffic Act 1988 and
- I do/do not have to wear seat belts under the Motor Vehicles (Wearing of Seat Belts) Regulations 1982.

Signed

Date

Centre	DEVONWOOD
Date	30.1. 2000
Make & model	FORD ESCORT
Reg Mark	N512 CTW

Dual Controls Fitted ✓ Not Fitted

Candidate's Name

Ref. No

Column A

PST No.7 Exercises 7P and 12T

Phase 1-7P Partly trained-Approaching junctions to turn either right or left

	Not Covered	Inadequately Covered	Adequately Covered
Briefing on approaching junctions	☐	☐	☐
Mirrors	☐	☐	☐
Signal	☐	☐	☐
Brakes	☐	☐	☐
Gears	☐	☐	☐
Coasting	☐	☐	☐
Too fast on approach	☐	☐	☐
Too slow on approach	☐	☐	☐
Position	☐	☐	☐
Pedestrians	☐	☐	☐
Cross approaching traffic	☐	☐	☐
Right corner cut	☐	☐	☐

Phase 2-12T Trained-Pedestrians crossings and the use of signals

	Not Covered	Inadequately Covered	Adequately Covered
Mirror-Signal-Manoeuvre	☐	☐	☐
Speed on approach	☐	☐	☐
Stop when necessary	☐	☐	☐
Overtaking on approach	☐	☐	☐
Inviting pedestrians to cross	☐	☐	☐
Signals by indicator	☐	☐	☐
Signals by arm	☐	☐	☐
Signals timing	☐	☐	☐
Unnecessary signals	☐	☐	☐

The results of your test are:

Phase I Grade   Phase II Grade

Supervising Examiner's name

Location   Section No.

S E Signature

Column B

In this column the top line of boxes to Phase I and the bottom line of boxes refer to Phase II

1/2/3 = Unsatisfactory   4/5/6 = Satisfactory

Core Competencies   1 2 3   4 5 6

Identification of faults

Fault analysis

Remedial action

Instructional Techniques   1 2 3   4 5 6

Level of instruction

Planning

Control of lesson

Communication

Q/A Techniques

Feedback/Encouragement

Instructor use of controls

Instructor Characteristics   1 2 3   4 5 6

Attitude and Approach to Pupil

ADI 26/PT/07 Rev 7/98

FORMS UK plc (C5176526800)

DRIVING STANDARDS AGENCY

Instructional Test - Part III

The Examiner has marked each aspect of your performance in columns A and B below. Please see overleaf for explanatory notes.

Register of Approved Driving Instructors (DSA)

Candidate's Declaration

I certify that
- the vehicle I have provided for the test is properly insured under the Road Traffic Act 1988 and
- I do/do not have to wear seat belts under the Motor Vehicles (Wearing of Seat Belts) Regulations 1982.

Signed

Date

Centre	DEVONWOOD
Date	30.1. 2000
Make & model	FORD ESCORT
Reg Mark	N512 CTW
Dual Controls	Fitted ✓ Not Fitted
Candidate's Name	
Ref. No	

Column A

PST No.8 Exercises 9P and 11T

Phase 1-9P Partly trained-T Junctions-Emerging

	Not Covered	Unsatisfactory	Satisfactory
Briefing on T junctions	☐	☐	☐
Mirror-signal-manoeuvre	☐	☐	☐
Speed	☐	☐	☐
Gears	☐	☐	☐
Coasting	☐	☐	☐
Observation	☐	☐	☐
Emerging	☐	☐	☐
Position right	☐	☐	☐
Position left	☐	☐	☐
Pedestrians	☐	☐	☐

Phase 2-11T Trained-Meet, cross and overtake other traffic allowing adequate clearance for other road users and anticipation

	Not Covered	Unsatisfactory	Satisfactory
Mirror-Signal-Manoeuvre	☐	☐	☐
Meet approaching traffic	☐	☐	☐
Cross approaching traffic	☐	☐	☐
Overtake other traffic	☐	☐	☐
Keep a safe distance	☐	☐	☐
Shaving other vehicles	☐	☐	☐
Anticipation of pedestrians	☐	☐	☐
Anticipation of cyclists	☐	☐	☐
Anticipation of drivers	☐	☐	☐

The results of your test are:

Phase I Grade

Phase II Grade

Supervising Examiner's name

Location

Section No.

S E Signature

Column B

In this column the top line of boxes to Phase I and the bottom line of boxes refer to Phase II

1/2/3 = Unsatisfactory   4/5/6 = Satisfactory

Core Competencies   1 2 3   4 5 6

- Identification of faults
- Fault analysis
- Remedial action

Instructional Techniques   1 2 3   4 5 6

- Level of instruction
- Planning
- Control of lesson
- Communication
- Q/A Techniques
- Feedback/Encouragement
- Instructor use of controls

Instructor Characteristics   1 2 3   4 5 6

- Attitude and Approach to Pupil

ADI 26/PT/08 Rev 7/98

FORMS UK plc FON13022349

Instructional Test - Part III

DRIVING STANDARDS AGENCY

The Examiner has marked each aspect of your performance in columns A and B below. Please see overleaf for explanatory notes.

Candidate's Declaration

I certify that
- the vehicle I have provided for the test is properly insured under the Road Traffic Act 1988 and
- I do/do not have to wear seat belts under the Motor Vehicles (Wearing of Seat Belts) Regulations 1982.

Signed

Date

Centre	DEVONWOOD
Date	30.1.2000
Make & model	FORD ESCORT
Reg Mark	N512 CTW

Dual Controls   Fitted ✓   Not Fitted

Candidate's Name

Ref. No

Column A

PST No.9 Exercises 10P and 12T

Phase 1 -10P Partly trained-Crossroads

	Not Covered	Unsatisfactory	Satisfactory
Briefing on crossroads	☐	☐	☐
Mirror-signal-manoeuvre	☐	☐	☐
Speed	☐	☐	☐
Gears	☐	☐	☐
Coasting	☐	☐	☐
Observation	☐	☐	☐
Emerging	☐	☐	☐
Position right	☐	☐	☐
Position left	☐	☐	☐
Pedestrians	☐	☐	☐
Cross approaching traffic	☐	☐	☐
Right corner cut	☐	☐	☐

Phase 2 -12T Trained-Pedestrian crossings and signals

	Not Covered	Unsatisfactory	Satisfactory
Mirror-Signal-Manoeuvre	☐	☐	☐
Speed on approach	☐	☐	☐
Stop when necessary	☐	☐	☐
Overtaking on approach	☐	☐	☐
Inviting pedestrians to cross	☐	☐	☐
Signals by indicator	☐	☐	☐
Signals by arm	☐	☐	☐
Signals timing	☐	☐	☐
Unnecessary signals	☐	☐	☐

The results of your test are:

Phase I Grade   Phase II Grade

Supervising Examiner's name

Location   Section No.

S E Signature

Column B

In this column the top line of boxes to Phase I and the bottom line of boxes refer to Phase II

1/2/3 = Unsatisfactory   4/5/6 = Satisfactory

Core Competencies

	1	2	3	4	5	6
Identification of faults						
Fault analysis						
Remedial action						

Instructional Techniques

	1	2	3	4	5	6
Level of instruction						
Planning						
Control of lesson						
Communication						
Q/A Techniques						
Feedback/Encouragement						
Instructor use of controls						

Instructor Characteristics

	1	2	3	4	5	6
Attitude and Approach to Pupil						

ADI 26/PT/09 Rev 7/98

FORMS UK plc PCN31662200

Instructional Test - Part III

DRIVING
STANDARDS
AGENCY

The Examiner has marked each aspect of your performance in columns A and B below. Please see overleaf for explanatory notes.

Candidate's Declaration

I certify that
- the vehicle I have provided for the test is properly insured under the Road Traffic Act 1988 and
- I do/do not have to wear seat belts under the Motor Vehicles (Wearing of Seat Belts) Regulations 1982.

Signed

Date

Centre	DEVONWOOD
Date	30.1.2000
Make & model	FORD ESCORT
Reg Mark	N512 CTW
Dual Controls	Fitted ✓ Not Fitted
Candidate's Name	
Ref. No	

Column A

PST No.10 Exercises 11P and 8T

Phase 1-11P Partly trained-Meet, cross and overtake other traffic allowing adequate clearance for other road users and anticipation

	Not Covered/ Incorrect	Unsatisfactory	Satisfactory
Briefing			
Mirror-signal-manoeuvre			
Meet approaching traffic			
Cross other traffic			
Overtaking other traffic			
Keep a safe distance			
Shaving other vehicles			
Anticipation of pedestrians			
Anticipation of cyclists			
Anticipation of drivers			

Phase 2-8T Trained-Progress / hesitancy - normal position

	Not Covered/ Incorrect	Unsatisfactory	Satisfactory
Progress too fast			
Progress too slow			
Hesitancy			
Normal position too wide from the left			
Normal position too close to the left			

The results of your test are:

Phase I Grade		Phase II Grade	

Supervising Examiner's name

Location ___ Section No. ___

S E Signature

Column B

In this column the top line of boxes to Phase I and the bottom line of boxes refer to Phase II

1/2/3 = Unsatisfactory   4/5/6 = Satisfactory

Core Competencies

	1 2 3	4 5 6
Identification of faults		
Fault analysis		
Remedial action		

Instructional Techniques

	1 2 3	4 5 6
Level of instruction		
Planning		
Control of lesson		
Communication		
Q/A Techniques		
Feedback/Encouragement		
Instructor use of controls		

Instructor Characteristics

	1 2 3	4 5 6
Attitude and Approach to Pupil		

ADI 26/PT/10 Rev 7/98

FORMS UK plc FC8170/21MB

Assessment Notes

The examiner has assessed your **overall performance** based on the markings shown in columns A and B. Using this measurement **a final assessment for each phase** has been made against the criteria below and these grades are shown at the foot of column A.

Criteria for Grading

6. Overall performance to a very high standard with no significant instructional weaknesses.

5. A good overall standard of instruction with some minor weakness in instructional technique.

4. A competent overall performance with some minor deficiencies in instructional technique.

3. An inadequate overall performance with some deficiencies in instructional technique.

2. A poor overall performance with numerous deficiencies in instructional technique.

1. Overall standard of instruction extremely poor or dangerous with incorrect or even dangerous instruction.

The minimum level for a PASS is a Grade 4 in each phase. You must achieve a satisfactory grade in each phase on the same occasion to obtain an overall pass in the examination.

Recommended Reading

There are some books available which may help you. In particular we recommend the following publications:

"Instructional Techniques and Practice for Driving Instructors" (2nd edition) by Les Walklin published by Stanley Thornes (Publishers) Ltd

"The Driving Instructors Handbook" by J Miller and Margaret Stacey published by Kogan Page; and

The Agency's Driving Manual and "The Driving Test". These can be obtained from The Stationery Office and most bookshops.

Appeals

You have no grounds to appeal against the examiner's decision just because you don't agree with it. But if you consider that your test was not properly conducted in accordance with the Regulations you may apply to a Magistrates Court in the area in which you reside (in Scotland to the Sheriff within whose jurisdiction you reside) which has power to determine this point. Should the Court find that the test was not properly conducted they may order a refund of the fee. (See Road Traffic Act 1988, Section 133).

You should note, however, that your right of appeal to the Court under section 133 is strictly limited to the question of whether the test was properly conducted in accordance with the Regulations.

Before you consider making any appeal you may wish to seek legal advice.

About the test

Following the initial greeting the examiner will ask

- to see your letter of appointment
- you to read, sign and date a declaration stating that the car you have provided complies with all the insurance regulations mentioned on your letter of appointment
- you to indicate below the declaration whether or not you are exempt from having to wear a seat belt
- if you have L plates or, if you wish, D plates in Wales.

Your letter of appointment may specify the name of the examiner. However, the Regulations state that the car **must be insured for any DSA staff examiner to drive.** This is because the person named on the letter of appointment may not be available on that day. In which case, another examiner will take the test. If the car has only been insured for one named examiner **your test will be cancelled, and you may lose your fee.**

The car must display L plates (or D plates). If you cannot provide them the test will be cancelled and you will lose the test fee. The examiner **may** allow you the opportunity to purchase a set if this can be done **in a reasonable time.**

Examiners work to a tight schedule and it is your responsibility to make sure that the vehicle you provide for the test meets all legal and other requirements.

It is worth remembering at this point that the car you provide must also meet the conditions stated on page 44. If it does not, **your test will be cancelled and you will lose your fee.**

When you have entered the car the examiner will inform you that

- this is the test of your ability to give instruction

- you should regard the examiner as your pupil and instruct in the way you would do normally.

It may be necessary to let you know when you have come to the end of each phase.

You will be given directions of the route – in both phases – in plenty of time so that you can think about them and repeat them back to the examiner, who will comply.

How the test is conducted

At the beginning of each phase, the examiner will 'set the scene' of the pupil he/she is about to role-play. You will be informed of the main subject(s) of the exercises you will be required to give instruction on, and you should correct any other faults that may occur.

In Phase I you will be asked to assume that the pupil is either a beginner or partly trained. In Phase II the examiner will play the part of a pupil at the trained stage – about driving-test standard.

Listen carefully to the subject(s) you will be asked to give instruction on and the description of the type of pupil the examiner intends to portray. If you are unsure about any of these details, ask the examiner for clarification before they go into role.

Phase I

The examiner will inform you that the role-play will be either that of

- a **complete beginner** who has never driven before and is on their first lesson

- a **beginner who has had one lesson** in which the instructor explained the controls but did not get round to moving off or stopping and (as a pupil) they are not sure when to use the mirrors. The car used on the previous lesson was the same as yours – this is to avoid time being lost explaining the location of the controls in a different car.

- a **partly trained pupil who has had a few lessons** and that the usual instructor is not able to give the lesson on that day, and the car they have been practising in is the same as yours and they are familiar with the controls – as previously mentioned, this is to avoid time being lost explaining the location of the controls in a different car.

It may not be convenient or suitable to start these particular exercises from outside some SE ADI offices.

In these circumstances, the examiner will ask you to assume that you have picked up the pupil from their place of work and drive to a suitable place.

You should consider that the lesson has started from the moment the examiner assumes the role of the pupil. You will be given directions and reminded that this is an instructional test and not a test of your own driving ability.

After approximately half an hour, the examiner will come out of role and inform you that Phase I is now over.

The examiner will then take a few minutes to make some notes before moving on to Phase II.

Phase II

Before making notes, the examiner will inform you of

- the subject of the lesson in Phase II

- the type of pupil they intend to role-play

- the level of the pupil's ability.

They will also remind you to correct any other faults worthy of note that may occur.

In Phase II you should consider the examiner as a totally different pupil. Don't make the mistake of assuming you have the same 'person' as portrayed in Phase I. That could be a recipe for failure.

After approximately a further half an hour, the examiner will come out of role and inform you that Phase II is over. They will take a few moments to make some notes, then inform you that the test is over.

The examiner will return to the office and complete the assessment and marking of your overall performance in both phases of the test.

This will be based on your

- method

- clarity

- adequacy

- correctness of instruction

- observation and correction of the pupil's driving errors

- attitude and approach.

A final assessment for each phase will be made and recorded in the box in column **A** which is headed 'The results of your test are:'

The Pre-Set Test (PST) papers

The main section of all the PST
marking papers are divided into two
columns headed A and B.

DSA
DRIVING
STANDARDS
AGENCY

Instructional Test - Part III

The Examiner has marked each aspect of your performance in
columns A and B below. Please see overleaf for explanatory notes.

Register of
Approved Driving
Instructors
(GB)

Candidate's Declaration

I certify that
- the vehicle I have provided for the test is properly insured under the Road Traffic Act 1988 and
- I do/do not have to wear seat belts under the Motor Vehicles (Wearing of Seat Belts) Regulations 1982.

Signed

Date

Centre

Date

Make & model

Reg Mark

Dual Controls   Fitted [ ]   Not Fitted [ ]

Candidate's Name

Ref. No

Column A

PST No.8 Exercises 9P and 11T

Phase 1-9P Partly trained-T Junctions-Emerging

	Not Covered	Unsatisfactory	Satisfactory
Briefing on T junctions	[ ]	[ ]	[ ]
Mirror-signal-manoeuvre	[ ]	[ ]	[ ]
Speed	[ ]	[ ]	[ ]
Gears	[ ]	[ ]	[ ]
Coasting	[ ]	[ ]	[ ]
Observation	[ ]	[ ]	[ ]
Emerging	[ ]	[ ]	[ ]
Position right	[ ]	[ ]	[ ]
Position left	[ ]	[ ]	[ ]
Pedestrians	[ ]	[ ]	[ ]

Phase 2-11T Trained-Meet, cross and overtake other traffic allowing adequate clearance for other road users and anticipation

	Not Covered	Unsatisfactory	Satisfactory
Mirror-Signal-Manoeuvre	[ ]	[ ]	[ ]
Meet approaching traffic	[ ]	[ ]	[ ]
Cross approaching traffic	[ ]	[ ]	[ ]
Overtake other traffic	[ ]	[ ]	[ ]
Keep a safe distance	[ ]	[ ]	[ ]
Shaving other vehicles	[ ]	[ ]	[ ]
Anticipation of pedestrians	[ ]	[ ]	[ ]
Anticipation of cyclists	[ ]	[ ]	[ ]
Anticipation of drivers	[ ]	[ ]	[ ]

The results of your test are:

Phase I Grade [   ]   Phase II Grade [   ]

Supervising Examiner's name

Location [   ]   Section No.

S E Signature

Column B

In this column the top line of boxes refer to Phase I and the bottom line of boxes refer to Phase II

1/2/3 = Unsatisfactory   4/5/6 = Satisfactory

Core Competencies

	1 2 3	4 5 6
Identification of faults		
Fault analysis		
Remedial action		

Instructional Techniques

	1 2 3	4 5 6
Level of instruction		
Planning		
Control of lesson		
Communication		
Q/A Techniques		
Feedback/Encouragement		
Instructor use of controls		

Instructor Characteristics

	1 2 3	4 5 6
Attitude and Approach to Pupil		

ADI 26/PT/08 Rev 7/98
FORMS UK plc FCH1/8072/00

Explanation of Column A

In Column **A**, Phases I and II are set out with Phase I in the top part of the column and Phase II in the lower.

The PST and exercise numbers are printed below the heading 'Column A'.

On the right of the exercise numbers are the letters B, P or T; they are abbreviations for

- Beginner
- Partly trained
- Trained.

These refer to the level of pupil ability role-played by the examiner.

For example

PST No.4 Exercises 3P and 9T

The PST number is 4, incorporating exercise 3 in the 'partly trained' stage at the top section of column A, and exercise 9 in the 'trained stage' lower down.

Below these numbers are the subjects of the lessons to be dealt with in each phase. In the example

Phase one = Partly trained – Reversing either to the left or right. (The examiner will state which.)

Phase two = Trained – T junctions – Emerging.

There are three separate rows of boxes headed

- 'Not covered'
- 'Unsatisfactory'
- 'Satisfactory'.

On the left of these boxes is a list of descriptions of the subject of the lesson. They vary in number depending on the PST.

As with Phase I, the subject items in Phase II are listed on the left below the lesson heading.

Column A

PST No.4 Exercises 3P and 9T

Phase 1-3P Partly trained-Reversing

Left Reverse ☐   Right Reverse ☐

	Not Covered	Unsatisfactory	Satisfactory
Briefing on reversing	☐	☐	☐
Co-ordination of controls	☐	☐	☐
Observation	☐	☐	☐
Accuracy	☐	☐	☐

Phase 2-9T Trained-T Junctions-Emerging

	Not Covered	Unsatisfactory	Satisfactory
Mirror-Signal-Manoeuvre	☐	☐	☐
Speed	☐	☐	☐
Gears	☐	☐	☐
Coasting	☐	☐	☐
Observation	☐	☐	☐
Emerging	☐	☐	☐
Position right	☐	☐	☐
Position left	☐	☐	☐

The examiner may decide to simulate faults applicable to all or just some of the subject items in each phase of column A. This will depend on the content of the PST, the main subject(s) of the exercises and/or the type of role-play and character they have chosen.

If the examiner decides not to simulate faults applicable to all of the subject items during either of the phases, those not simulated would be ruled through and not included in the overall assessment.

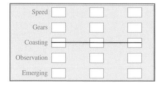

The examiner will take into account the assessment and marking of both phases in this column before arriving at the overall grade of each phase. Each subject item in both phases will be assessed and marked under one of the headings.

Not Covered Failure to identify any faults simulated and applicable to the subject items in either phase will be recorded by means of a diagonal line in the box under this heading against the subject item(s).

For example, if the examiner simulates a 'Coasting' fault in the 'Trained stage' of 'T-junctions – Emerging' and it is neither identified nor mentioned by you, the examiner, when assessing the test, will insert a diagonal line in the box headed 'Not Covered' against the subject item 'Coasting'.

Phase 2-9T Trained-T Junctions-Emerging			
	Not Covered	Unsatisfactory	Satisfactory
Mirror-Signal-Manoeuvre			
Speed			
Gears			
Coasting	/		

Unsatisfactory If you identify the fault, but the instruction and/or correction given is either inaccurate or incomplete, it will be recorded by a diagonal line in the box under this heading against the subject item(s).

Satisfactory If the fault is identified and you give satisfactory instruction and guidance to prevent it being repeated, the examiner will record this with a diagonal line under this heading against the subject item(s).

Explanation of column B

The information in Column B on each PST states 'In this column the top line of boxes refers to Phase I and the bottom line of boxes refers to Phase II'.

Below this statement are the numbers used in a six point rating scale, shown as

- 1/2/3 = Unsatisfactory
- 4/5/6 = Satisfactory

The column is set out in three separate sections which accommodates a rating scale for each phase under the sub-headings

- Core competencies
- Instructional Techniques
- Instructor Characteristics

These sections are broken down into specific subjects which, when individually assessed and marked, will reflect the strengths and/or weaknesses of your instructional ability. As with Column A, the marks are recorded by means of a diagonal line.

When marking subjects in column B, every box will be marked according to the examiner's assessment of the ratings. There is however, one exception, that is the 'Instructor's use of controls'. If you do not use any of the controls, the rating scale appropriate to that phase would be ruled through with a single line.

Column B
In this column the top line of boxes to Phase I and the bottom line of boxes refer to Phase II

1/2/3 = Unsatisfactory   4/5/6 = Satisfactory

Core Competencies

	1 2 3	4 5 6
Identification of faults		
Fault analysis		
Remedial action		

Instructional Techniques

	1 2 3	4 5 6
Level of instruction		
Planning		
Control of lesson		
Communication		
Q/A Techniques		
Feedback/Encouragement		
Instructor use of controls		

Instructor Characteristics

	1 2 3	4 5 6
Attitude and Approach to Pupil		

Feedback/Encouragement		
Instructor use of controls		

Core competencies

There are three core competencies that form the basis of good instruction. They are

- fault identification
- fault analysis
- remedial action.

While waiting for faults to occur may be necessary, more benefit can be obtained by anticipating a pupil's actions and dealing with them positively in advance.

You must correctly identify, analyse and remedy weaknesses to improve a pupil's driving skills.

Fault identification

The examiner will assess your ability to identify and prioritise weaknesses in the pupil's performance.

You must switch between observation of the pupil and what is happening outside of the car. The pupil can be observed directly and with the use of strategically placed mirrors.

For example, you ask the pupil to pull up on the left just past the next lamp-post.

If the procedure is observed to be carried out correctly, there is no fault. However, if the sequence is wrong, incorrectly timed or there is an omission in procedure, then the pupil needs to be told. If they are not told that a fault has occurred, the examiner would assess it accordingly.

Having identified whether or not faults have been made, your attention should revert to what is happening outside.

Fault analysis

Faults in either procedure or control which have been identified and brought to the pupil's attention should be analysed as to why they have occurred.

For example, when making a left turn from a major into a minor road, the near-side rear wheel may mount the kerb.

There are several reasons why this could happen, such as the pupil

- being too close to the kerb on the approach
- turning the wheel to the left too soon.

It's up to you as a trainee driving instructor to correctly analyse the cause and explain what went wrong.

Remedial action

Having **identified** and **analysed** the fault, the pupil will now need to know how to avoid repeating it – **the remedy.**

This should be given at the earliest opportunity. You should explain how the fault can be corrected and what might have happened because of the pupil's actions. Your explanation should be concise and fully understood. Following the explanation, you should consider consolidating the theory with practice.

Try to avoid leaving it for any length of time as, in reality, it is unlikely that you would be able to rely on the pupil's memory of events. Late or retrospective instruction is of little value. The pupil should not be expected to have the detailed recall of an experienced driver.

Instructional techniques

These are the tools available to structure the lesson and ensure there is an opportunity for learning to take place.

This section is broken down into seven subject headings.

- Level of instruction.
- Planning.
- Control of lesson.
- Communication.
- Question and answer techniques.
- Feedback/encouragement.
- Instructor's use of controls.

Level of instruction

This relates to the match (or lack of it) between the level of your instruction and the level of ability of the pupil described and portrayed by the examiner.

You will need to judge effectively, from the description and the pupil's driving ability, at what level you should be instructing. For the levels to be well matched, you will need to build on the strengths and focus on areas which need further development. The lesson should be adjusted accordingly, concentrating on the pupil's needs.

The pupil's level of ability will dictate the level of instruction.

The skill in successfully matching these levels is knowing when to instruct and when to keep quiet. It is likely, in the novice and partly trained stages, or if the lesson is dealing with a new subject, that you will initially need to talk the pupil through each stage.

When teaching a new skill using the 'talk through' method, it is important that the instruction is correct, concise and is given at the right level so that success is achieved at the first attempt.

When using this method, allow enough time for the pupil to interpret and carry out your instructions.

You should adjust the level and amount of instruction to suit the needs and ability of the pupil. If a fault remains evident despite attempts to correct it, you may need to consider adapting your method of instruction to suit the pupil's level of ability and understanding. Detailed instruction should decrease as the pupil's level of ability increases. There are several reasons why the level of instruction may not match the ability of the pupil. However, the two most common are

- over-instruction
- under-instruction.

Over-instruction If you never stop talking and telling the pupil what to do and how to do it, you will find it very difficult to assess

- what they are thinking
- their progress
- the effectiveness of your instruction.

You must display the ability to transfer responsibility for problem-solving and decision-making to the pupil at the appropriate time. This will help you identify what the pupil already knows and, more importantly, what they need to know. It will also create the opportunity for you to assess the effectiveness of your instruction and the pupil's progress.

Examples of over-instruction would be if you were constantly telling a 'pupil' in the 'trained stage' (Phase II) how to recognise the clutch 'biting point', when to change gear, how to brake, etc. Instruction given at an elementary level in Phase II would be assessed as a mis-match against the pupil's level of ability and marked as 'unsatisfactory'.

Under-instruction Quite simply this means instruction or guidance was needed but was incomplete. Allowing novice or partly trained pupils to struggle through situations with little or no guidance is not good instruction and, in reality, could be dangerous.

Saying very little and/or just listing faults and then pulling up at the side of the road to discuss them is of very little value and would be assessed as retrospective instruction. Identifying faults but failing to give analysis and/or remedial guidance are other prime examples. Likewise, if the analysis and/or remedial guidance were incomplete, it would be of little value and marked as 'unsatisfactory'.

For example, if the rear wheel mounted the kerb when making a left turn, you should

- inform the pupil that the fault has occurred
- look at the reasons for it happening
- give correct guidance to prevent it being repeated.

If there is a short-fall in any one or more of these aspects, you have under-instructed and will be assessed accordingly.

Planning

The lesson should be structured and presented in an orderly manner following a clear and logical pattern. Account should be taken of the complexity of the subject(s) to be covered. You should consider the allocation of time between theory and practice.

Briefings should be exactly what the word suggests – brief. Try to avoid too much stationary instruction as, realistically, there is only so much verbal information a pupil can take in and understand at any one time. The lesson and your teaching methods should be linked to the pupil's ability.

Any visual aids, diagrams or reference material should, where possible, be prepared and close to hand ready to use. Avoid reading out sections of text, as this casts doubt on your knowledge of subject matter and also limits pupil involvement.

Failing to plan is planning to fail.

Control of the lesson

It's important that you relate control of the lesson to the characteristics and driving ability of the pupil the examiner has described. You must be able to anticipate the unexpected and be aware of what is going on outside, as well as inside the car.

The examiner will assess your awareness and perception of any changes either inside or outside of the car. You must demonstrate the ability to anticipate and take appropriate action to deal with any potential errors or dangers. This should include the ability to prioritise in different situations, particularly approaching and/or dealing with various hazards.

The timing of your instruction is important and should be linked to pupil ability. Intervening too soon will prevent you from knowing whether or not the pupil was going to react and in what way. If you leave it too late, your instruction may have to be hurried and become confusing. In reality this might result in a dangerous situation.

The ability to prioritise is essential.

Here is a scenario.

The pupil passes rather close to a parked vehicle.

Whilst correcting this fault, you are approaching on-coming traffic in a narrowing section of road.

There is only enough room for one vehicle at a time to drive through safely.

You are now heading towards a non-existent gap and time is running out.

It should be obvious that the priority in this scenario is 'meeting approaching traffic' and it should be treated as such. If you continue to instruct on how to pass stationary vehicles safely and ignore the approaching hazard, you are not dealing with the priority at that time.

Having yourself identified potential hazards, you will need to judge the pupil's awareness of situations and establish how they are likely to react.

Communication

Good two-way communication is important if learning is to take place. Your delivery of instruction and correction should be fluent and easy to understand, using simple terminology. Avoid unnecessary use of jargon, and if it does become necessary, make sure the pupil has understood.

When you are talking to the pupil you should be watching for facial expressions such as frowning. This may indicate a lack of understanding of what is being said. Be prepared to adapt and make adjustments to your style if you think the pupil does not understand you.

Directions should be given clearly and at the appropriate time. Avoid any ambiguity or misunderstanding. The examiner's directions on route will be given in time for you to think before repeating them back. This creates the opportunity for the examiner to assess your ability to time and deliver directions.

The question and answer (Q and A) session

The power of effective questioning as an aid to learning is sometimes overlooked. Basically, there are four reasons for asking questions.

- To motivate a pupil by gaining their interest and attention.
- To promote mental activity.
- To involve the pupil as a partner in the instructional process.
- To establish a starting point and confirm the pupil's understanding and recall of what they have learned, i.e., what they already know and what they need to know.

Instruction is a a two way process where the instructor may, at times, become the recipient of a question. Any questions or queries raised by the pupil should be fully and correctly answered. The pupil should be encouraged to ask questions or raise queries whenever they feel it necessary.

When considering the use of Q and A, you should

- be able to judge whether the questions are appropriate in relation to the lesson
- balance the weight and complexity of the question to match the ability of the pupil
- be sure that the questions are testing and/or thought provoking

- be sure you use the questions effectively to
  - recap on a lesson
  - prompt the pupil
  - establish their knowledge
  - encourage pupil participation.

Make sure you allow the pupil time to respond. Avoid questions about situations that occurred some time previously. This may be assessed as retrospective instruction which usually is of little value to the pupil.

Types of question to be considered

There are two types of question most frequently used; these are – 'open' and 'closed'.

Closed questions   These are of limited value and can usually be answered with a single word.

There are two types of closed questions. Those that

- can be answered with either a 'yes' or a 'no', such as
  - can you drive?
  - is this your car?

- ask for a specific piece of information, such as
  - where do you work?
  - how many lessons have you had?

Asking questions that only require a 'yes' or 'no' or one word answer is unlikely to establish what the pupil is thinking or understands. Questions that ask for a specific piece of information are little more than a test of memory. Closed questions contribute very little to the learning process.

Open questions   These types of questions can be searching, thought provoking and challenging. They do not limit the content of an answer.

To benefit both you, and the pupil, questions are of more value if they are formulated around the words 'what', 'why', 'how', 'where', 'when' and 'who'.

'What' are the dangers of following too close to the vehicle in front?

'Why' should you apply, as a minimum, the 'two second rule'?

'How' do you apply the 'two second rule' when following behind other traffic?

'Where' should you be looking to identify other potential dangers when following in traffic?

'When' would you consider doubling the 'two second rule'.

'Who' else may affect your decision to increase separation distance?

These examples show how you can use the words, and are **not a definitive method of how to deal with separation distance.**

Two types of questions you should generally avoid using are

• trick questions

• elliptical questions.

Trick questions usually show off the knowledge of the instructor and are of no value to the pupil.

Elliptical questions are those in which the pupil is meant to fill in the missing word(s). They can take the form of incomplete sentences. For example

Before you give a signal you should check the------------?

This type of question is also of little use. It encourages single word replies and is more like a guessing game.

The Q and A session, as with other instructional techniques, should be used when it is the most appropriate method of dealing with a problem and will enhance the pupil's learning skills. **It is not the 'be all and end all' of giving instruction – as some people think.**

Overloading the pupil with a flood of questions is not good instruction. In reality, it can be very tiring and distracting, and sometimes demoralising, particularly if they cannot answer the questions correctly.

Feedback and encouragement

These techniques can be very valuable instructional tools. The examiner will assess your ability to provide feedback and give encouragement during each phase. Giving praise and encouragement can be a good confidence booster.

It's important to keep the pupil updated on their level of achievement. This will provide them with a realistic measure of how they are progressing and keep them motivated. Gaining feedback from the pupil is just as important as giving it. A good instructor will be able to recognise uncertainties or insecurities in the pupil through

- body language
- facial expressions, including eye contact
- the spoken word

and react in a positive manner.

You should respond with appropriate advice and guidance. Avoid ambiguous or confusing feedback.

It's important to gain information from the pupil about how they think they are progressing. This will help you decide whether or not you need to adjust the level of your instruction. Feedback from the pupil could come in the form of questions, which you should promote.

For example, if the pupil asks 'Do I have priority at the next junction?' you need to establish why the pupil is uncertain. If you just answer 'yes' or 'no', the only learning that will take place is that the pupil will now know that

- at that particular junction
- when approaching it from that particular direction

they either have, or have not, got priority; they need to know and understand *why*.

In the novice or partly trained stage, praise and encouragement may prove effective for the most basic of achievements. However, in the trained stage, praise for similar levels of basic achievement might be considered inappropriate and patronising.

When giving praise, it should reflect the true performance level achieved and/or displayed. To say something was 'well done' or 'excellent' when in fact it was only satisfactory is not a true reflection.

Use simple and appropriate language; the use of superlatives, in most instances, exaggerates the true level of achievement and/or performance.

Avoid using words or phrases such as 'mega', 'fantastic', 'brilliant', 'absolutely splendid', etc.

Instructors use of controls

The instructor should only make use of the controls to

- give a demonstration
- avoid a *potentially* dangerous situation
- avoid a situation involving *actual* danger.

If it becomes necessary for the instructor to use any of the controls the pupil should be told why. Use of the controls means *all* controls, such as

- the dual clutch, brake or accelerator (if fitted)
- the handbrake
- the gear selector
- the steering wheel
- the driver's sun-visor
- the wipers and washers
- the direction indicators
- the heaters, demisters or heated rear window
- the lights
- the horn
- the electric windows (if fitted).

It's important to ensure that the level of instruction matches the needs of the pupil to avoid unnecessary use of the controls.

For example, you've asked the pupil to pull up at the side of the road but they mis-judge the position on approach, and begin to steer on a collision course towards the kerb.

It's far more effective to react early by giving verbal instruction, than suddenly grabbing the steering wheel or using the dual controls at the last moment.

A direct link can be made between the subject items, 'Instructors use of controls' and 'Control of the lesson'. There should be very little need for the instructor to use the controls or take physical action if the lesson is under control.

Conversely, if the instructor is controlling the lesson by using the controls, what is the pupil being taught?

Instructor characteristics

Attitude and approach to the pupil

It's vitally important that you create a friendly learning environment if you are to get the best from your pupil. You should have the ability to recognise the type of person you are teaching and adjust your approach accordingly.

Patience and tact should be applied at all times. If the pupil does not get it right the first time, be prepared to repeat the information/instruction, or look for the next opportunity to deal with that topic again.

There should be no need for any physical contact other than shaking hands during introduction. Physical contact can be mis-construed and is often resented. Clear instruction will alleviate any need for it.

You should be your usual self and instruct in the way you would normally. There should only be one actor in the car. If you attempt to be someone you are not, or change your normal method of instruction, you may find it difficult to sustain for an hour and lose your concentration – **be yourself and have less to think about.**

The examiner's assessment

To pass the Part Three test, the minimum grade **in each phase** must be **at least** 4.

Grade 5 achieved in the Phase I

but only

Grade 3 in the Phase II

would result in an overall failure to pass the examination.

As previously stated, the examiner marks each aspect of your performance in columns A and B with one single diagonal line in the appropriate boxes.

There is no connection whatsoever between the assessment and marking of Phases I and II. They are assessed and marked individually and are considered as two completely different 'lessons'.

There are positive links between columns A and B and also between the various instructional techniques, in the overall assessment and grading of each phase. The examiner will take these into consideration when assessing and marking the quality of instruction given.

The following is an example and only one scenario exemplifying how these markings may be interlinked.

If your fault identification was weak throughout a phase, this could result in

- a 'not covered' or 'unsatisfactory' mark in one or more of the subject items in column A
- an unsatisfactory rating of the **'Identification of faults'** in column B (A rating of 3, 2 or 1 depending on the severity of weakness)
- other aspects of **'Instructional techniques'** being rated at an unsatisfactory level.

Consider the knock-on effects and implications in this.

Level of instruction A lack of ability to identify faults would result in a mismatch between the level of instruction and the level of the pupil's ability. Failure to identify faults, in reality, would hinder a pupil's progress as they would be unaware of their incorrect actions.

Planning How could the lesson be well planned to suit the needs of the pupil if many faults were uncorrected?

Instructional Test - Part III

The Examiner has marked each aspect of your performance in columns A and B below. Please see overleaf for explanatory notes.

DRIVING STANDARDS AGENCY

Candidate's Declaration

I certify that
- the vehicle I have provided for the test is properly insured under the Road Traffic Act 1988 and
- I do/do not have to wear seat belts under the Motor Vehicles (Wearing of Seat Belts) Regulations 1982.

Signed _Apunger Allen_

Date 30.1.2000

Centre	DEVONWOOD
Date	30.1.2000
Make & model	FORD ESCORT
Reg Mark	N512 CTW
Dual Controls	Fitted ☑ Not Fitted
Candidate's Name	MR H GRAINGER-ALLAN
Ref. No	17791

Column A

PST No.4 Exercises 3P and 9T

Phase 1-3P Partly trained-Reversing

Left Reverse ☑   Right Reverse ☐

	Not Covered	Unsatisfactory	Satisfactory
Briefing on reversing			☑
Co-ordination of controls		☑	
Observation	☑		
Accuracy		☑	

Phase 2-9T Trained-T Junctions-Emerging

	Not Covered	Unsatisfactory	Satisfactory
Mirror-Signal-Manoeuvre			
Speed			
Gears			
Coasting			
Observation			
Emerging			
Position right			
Position left			
Pedestrians			

The results of your test are:

Phase I Grade **2**   Phase II Grade

Supervising Examiner's name

Location   Section No.

S E Signature

Column B

In this column the top line of boxes to Phase I and the bottom line of boxes refer to Phase II

1/2/3 = Unsatisfactory   4/5/6 = Satisfactory

Core Competencies

	1	2	3	4	5	6
Identification of faults		☑				
Fault analysis	☑					
Remedial action	☑					

Instructional Techniques

	1	2	3	4	5	6
Level of instruction		☑				
Planning	☑					
Control of lesson					☑	
Communication	☑					
Q/A Techniques					☑	
Feedback/Encouragement	☑					
Instructor use of controls					☑	

Instructor Characteristics

	1	2	3	4	5	6
Attitude and Approach to Pupil					☑	

ADI 26/PT/04 Rev 7/98

FORMS UK plc

Control of the lesson   If situations were allowed to develop which required you to take panic action either verbally or by using the controls, this would reflect in the assessment of the control of the lesson.

Feedback and encouragement
This could be incorrect, incomplete or inaccurate as you are only partly aware of what is going on.

Instructor's use of controls (if used)   Possibly could have been avoided had the fault been identified and the necessary guidance given earlier.

It can be seen in the example that, because of a weakness in ability to identify faults, there are knock-on effects to the ratings of other aspects that affect the overall assessment.

There are an infinite number of situations that result in different combinations of marking and assessment of these tests. No two tests are ever the same, simply because of the constantly-changing road and traffic situations and conditions.

It is, therefore, of little value trying to duplicate or mimic a Pre-Set Test (PST) that you may have practised with your trainer. The test is designed to check your overall potential ability as an instructor not just the quality of one particular type of lesson that may have been rehearsed, such as the 'Turn in the road' exercise.

The result

The results are sent to you on the same day as your test. A copy of the test report will be enclosed.

What to do if you fail

If you are unsuccessful, providing you are still within your two-year maximum time limit and have not used up all three attempts, you may re-apply by completing the application form on the reverse side of the letter informing you of the result. Send it with the appropriate fee to DSA headquarters.

As previously stated, if you fail the Part Three on the third attempt, you must wait until your two-year period has lapsed before re-applying to take the three qualifying tests again.

Likewise, if you fail the test on your first or second attempt and your two-year period has lapsed, you will not be allowed a further attempt and will have to start again at the beginning.

What to do if you pass

If you are successful, you can apply for entry onto the Register of Approved Driving Instructors (Car) by completing the application form on the reverse side of the letter informing you of the result. Send it, with two passport size photographs and the appropriate fee, to DSA headquarters.

You should receive a green Certificate of Registration by post, within one week of your application being received at DSA headquarters. It will have affixed to it one of the passport photographs.

The certificate also records your name, your ADI Personal Reference Number and the dates of issue and expiry. It's valid for a period of four years.

The Regulations specify that, whenever you are charging for a lesson, your ADI certificate must be fixed to, and immediately behind the front windscreen of the car you are teaching in. It should be displayed on the nearside edge of the screen so that the particulars on the back are clearly visible from the outside. The particulars on the front must be clearly visible from the nearside front seat.

Your responsibilities

You can now apply for entry into a profession that offers very worthwhile tuition in an important subject. No doubt you have worked very hard and invested much time and money to gain this qualification. It's important to maintain and build upon the standards you demonstrated both in your own driving and your ability to give instruction.

This is not the time to sit back and relax. You must keep yourself up-to-date with changes in the law and any other developments affecting your new profession.

You will become a member of a relatively small group of people who make a significant contribution to the quality of driving on our roads today.

"Safe driving for life"

Stanley House
Talbot Street
Nottingham
NG1 5GU.

Your personal ref No

Date

Dear Candidate

Register of Approved Driving Instructors

I am glad to tell you that you reached the approved standard in your recent test of instructional ability, which is the final part of the Register qualifying examination.

Provided that you still satisfy the other conditions of registration your name may be entered in the register and a Certificate of Registration issued to you. To enable us to proceed with your application for registration will you please answer the questions and sign the declaration overleaf.

You should then return this completed letter together with the fee for registration and two passport type photographs to the above address. Cheques etc should be crossed and made payable to "Driving Standards Agency".

It is important that you let the Registrar's office know if you change your address whilst you are on the Register.

When completing the declaration overleaf, you will notice a section referring to release of information. We are frequently approached by outside organisations, including the associations which represent driving instructors, asking for names and addresses on our database, but before we can supply any information, we are obliged under the Data Protection Act 1984 to ask you for your consent.

Would you therefore please tick one of the boxes to indicate whether or not you wish your name and address to be released. If you give your consent, we would make it a condition that organisations would not, in turn, sell it to someone else. If you tick box 'F' this means that you are content for your name and address to be released to any company or organisation. A tick in box 'P' means that you are content for your name and address to be released to companies or organisations in the field of driving instruction only, and a tick in box 'N' means that you do not wish your name and address to be released to any company or organisation but you will still receive mailings from the Driving Standards Agency.

We would also like to invite you to indicate your ethnic origin. This will help us to ensure that discrimination does not take place. We hope you will provide the information, but this is completely voluntary.

Yours faithfully

Supervising Examiner
Register of Approved Driving Instructors.

ADI 12 (11/92

Declaration

Tick appropriate box

1 Since the date you applied for registration have you been disqualified from driving, or have you any endorsements on your driving licence?

Yes ☐ No ☐

2 Since the date you applied for registration have you been convicted of a non-motoring offence?

Yes ☐ No ☐

3 Are Court proceedings of any kind pending against you?

Yes ☐ No ☐

Note: If you have answered 'yes' to any of the above questions please give precise details and dates of offences committed, dates of offences, court attended and penalties imposed.

4 What will be your business address and the name of the business establishment?

Postcode   Telephone No

5 In what area(s) will you work as an ADI? (ie the nearest large town or part of a city.)

Release of Information:
Please tick one of the following boxes.

F ☐   P ☐   N ☐

Ethnic Origin:
Please tick one of the following boxes:

White ☐   Pakistani ☐   Black-African ☐   Black-Caribbean ☐   Black-Other ☐
Bangladeshi ☐   Chinese ☐   Indian ☐   Other ☐

- I declare that the details given on this document are to the best of my knowledge true and correct.
- I confirm that I will inform the Registrar within 7 days if I am convicted of any offence including motoring offences.
- I confirm that I will present myself for 'check tests' when required to do so by the Registrar.
- I enclose two passport type photographs for use in my Certificate of Registration and the registration fee of £ ☐ for the entry of my name in the Register of Approved Driving Instructors.

Signature ☐   Date ☐

The topics covered

- How the Check Test is arranged
- About the test
- Core competencies
- Instructional techniques
- Instructor characteristics
- Overall marking and assessment
- The grading system
- The result

The Check Test is the test of your continued ability and fitness to give instruction.

The Road Traffic Act 1988 lays down that registration is subject to the condition that an ADI will undergo a Check Test at any time required by the Registrar. The requirement to have a Check Test every so often is, therefore, a statutory one.

When you have qualified to become an Approved Driving Instructor (Car) and had your name entered on the Register, the SE for your local area will receive this information and open up a personal file in your name.

This file will contain details of your home and driving school addresses and telephone numbers. It will also contain copies of Check Test invitations, your replies, copies of your Check Test reports and any correspondence of a general nature applicable to yourself. The results of your past and current gradings are also kept on record at DSA headquarters.

The Check Test is conducted by an SE who will accompany you on a normal lesson with a pupil. The SE sits in the back of the car and checks that you are maintaining, at least, the minimum standard of instruction required to remain on the Register of Approved Driving Instructors (Car).

However, a review is currently being conducted into how instructors are trained and tested. One of the options under consideration is that of using role play (as Part Three) to assess an ADI's performance on the Check Test.

After the Check Test the SE will give constructive guidance on the way instruction can be improved and/or to offer help and advice should it fall below the required standard. You can also make use of the time available after the test to discuss any specific items with the SE.

Many instructors admit to being unnerved by the Check Test, whilst others take a much more positive view. They welcome the opportunity to have their instructional ability re-assessed and look forward to receiving any necessary guidance and information from the SE.

Your overall instructional ability is assessed and graded according to the standards laid down by DSA, Grade 1 being the lowest and Grade 6 the highest. Grades 1, 2 and 3 are unsatisfactory and Grades 4, 5 and 6 are satisfactory.

Some enthusiastic ADIs look upon the check test as an opportunity to try and better their present grade.

The grading system will be dealt with in more detail later in this section.

How the Check Test is arranged

Each month the SE receives a computer print-out from DSA headquarters.

The print-out contains a list of ADIs in that SE's area, arranged in priority order to be seen for Check Test. It shows

- your name
- your personal reference number (PRN)
- your ADI licence expiry date
- the date and grade of your last Check Test (where applicable).

It also contains details of the most recent information up-date you have supplied to DSA; e.g., the name of the driving school you are currently working with or the name of your driving school and changes of address and telephone numbers – private and business (where applicable).

You must inform DSA headquarters as soon as possible, of any change of home and/or works address and telephone number(s).

A lot of time and resources are wasted trying to trace ADIs who, through lack of thought, fail to up-date DSA with a change of particulars.

As an **Approved Driving Instructor, you will have signed a declaration agreeing to inform the Registrar's office, in writing, within seven days of any change in your details or conviction for any offence, including any motoring offences. Failure to comply with these regulations could lead to removal of your name from the Register.**

You will appreciate that to keep the ADI registration fee as low as possible, it is vital that the SE's time is used economically.

The SE completes a pre-printed invitation – Form ADI 40 – and sends it with a stamped addressed envelope enclosed for you to use when replying. Also enclosed is a copy of Form ADI 40E. This is a leaflet which gives a brief outline about the check test for your information.

ADI 40 (Rev 10/95)

DRIVING STANDARDS AGENCY

Register of Approved Driving Instructors

ADI No _____

Date _____

Dear Instructor

Tests of continued ability and fitness to give instruction (check tests)

1   As you knew it is a condition of your continued registration as an Approved Driving Instructor that you will undergo a check test when required to do so. I have therefore arranged to travel to your area to conduct a check test on: -

Date_____ Time_____

Place_____

Please arrange for a normal lesson of approximately one hour to begin at the time shown and attend with a car and pupil. You should allow up to 15 minutes for discussion at the end of this lesson and, therefore, it should not be a lesson which is immediately followed by a driving test. I attach information about the check test which I hope you will find useful.

2   Please complete and return the detachable part of this letter to me confirming that you will be able to attend this appointment. This should reach me fully completed by return of post in the envelope provided. If you do not return it, or if you cannot attend without good reason on this date then you will be required to attend with a pupil at my office at a time and date arranged by the Registrar. If you think that you may have difficulty attending please read the attached notes (ADI40(E)), particularly the paragraph headed "The Invitation".

3   If, due to unforeseen circumstances I am, at the last moment, prevented from attending the appointment, you should proceed with the lesson in the usual way. If this happens I will contact you and make fresh arrangements. Should you be unable to keep this appointment at the last moment, then please telephone me as soon as possible so that alternative arrangements can be made. I am usually in the office on Fridays, and you can also leave messages on my answerphone on _____.

4   *I have to advise you that failure to attend for your check test could lead to your name being removed from the Register.*

Yours Sincerely

Supervising Examiner ADI

- -

I acknowledge receipt of your letter dated _____

*   I will attend for a check test on: Date _____ Time _____ Place _____

*   I have decided not to attend for a check test and return my Certificate of Registration

*   Exceptional circumstances prevent me from attending for the check test appointment (please explain why overleaf and supply evidence to support your claim eg: medical certificate or hospital appointment card)

(* Delete as appropriate)

Signed _____   Name of Driving School _____

Name _____   Vehicle to be used _____

Date _____ ADI No. _____   Registration No. _____

Home telephone No. _____

THE CHECK TEST

What You Should Know

Issued by the Registrar of Approved Driving Instructors July 1990

Test Of Continued Ability And Fitness To Give Instruction

Introduction

The Road Traffic Act 1988 (formerly the Road Traffic Act 1972) lays down that continued registration is subject to the condition that the ADI will undergo a check test at any time required by the Registrar. The requirement to have a check test every so often is a statutory one.

The things on which the ADI's lesson is judged are laid down in Regulations made under the Act and are referred to later in this paper under 'The Result'.

The check test is basically no more than its name suggests:-

an opportunity for your Supervising Examiner (SE) to check, by accompanying you while you conduct a normal lesson, that your instruction is up to the level required for you to remain on the ADI Register.

Nevertheless experience has shown that many instructors have misconceptions about what is required, and these often make it more difficult for your SE to assess an Instructor's true ability.

Please read, and heed, the following advice.

The Invitation

Normally, your SE will write to you at your home address. He/she will indicate the time and place for your appointment which is normally local to the area in which you work - often the local Driving Test Centre. It is important that you attend for the check test unless it is impossible for you to do so. In any event please return the acknowledgement slip as soon as possible.

You will appreciate that to keep the ADI registration fee as low as possible it is vital that the SE's time is used as economically as possible. ADIs who do not turn up for their appointments waste the SE's time and can put their own registration in jeopardy. Clearly there will be occasions when it is accepted that an ADI will be unable to attend for the check test eg on holiday, hospital appointment, long term illness. If that is the case please provide your SE with a copy of the holiday booking form, appointment card or doctor's note and he will arrange another appointment.

ADI 40(E)
(Rev 11/97)

Last Printed Feb'98

If possible, within the first 12 months of initial Registration, your SE will send you an invitation to attend your first Check Test.

If you have been on the Register for some time and have attended for a Check Test at least once, the grade you attained on the most recent Check Test will be a contributory factor in determining when you will receive a subsequent invitation.

Normally, the SE will send the invitation to your home address giving you several weeks notice of the Check Test appointment. They will indicate the date, time and place which is local to the area in which you normally work – more often than not the local Driving Test Centre.

On the bottom of the invitation there is a 'tear-off' acknowledgement slip. It's important that you attend the Check Test unless it is impossible for you to do so. In any event, you should return the acknowledgement slip, in the stamped addressed envelope provided, stating whether or not you will be attending, by return of post. If you can't attend, you must write on the back of the slip your reason for non-attendance.

Obviously there are occasions when it will be accepted that you will be unable to attend for the Check Test, e.g., if you are on holiday, if you have a hospital appointment, if you are ill, etc. In these circumstances, you must provide the SE with a copy of your holiday booking form, your appointment card or a doctor's note, and send it by return with the acknowledgement slip. The SE will then postpone your test to a later date.

It's not sufficient to just telephone the SE or leave a message on the answer-phone with a reason for non-attendance. The acknowledgement slip and any evidence supporting your reason *must* be sent by return to the SE.

ADIs who do not turn up for their appointments put their registration in jeopardy as well as wasting the SE's time.

Unacceptable reasons for non-attendance are

- not having a pupil
- not working as an ADI at the moment
- not having a car.

It may be that you do not have a pupil, and/or you are not currently offering driving tuition. In these circumstances you could try to borrow a pupil from another ADI. If this is not possible, it is acceptable for you to give a lesson to a full licence holder who may be a friend, colleague, member of your family, etc. However, the content and instruction offered must be commensurate with that person's ability – in other words you must not give a 'learner' lesson to a full licence holder.

To avoid any possibility of collusion, **it's not acceptable to have another ADI acting as your pupil**. Apart from any other consideration, if a qualified ADI required tuition, it would put *their* credibility at stake as a professional driver.

If you don't have a car, it may be possible for you to hire one for a few hours from a local driving school.

It's your responsibility to take whatever steps are necessary to make yourself available with a pupil and a car at the appointed time and place. **Failure to do so leaves you open to removal from the Register.**

If, due to unforeseen circumstances, at the last moment, the SE is prevented from attending they will make sure that you are contacted and make alternative arrangements for another date.

About the test

The vehicle

The vehicle must be roadworthy, safe and reliable. It should have L plates (or D plates) if you are teaching a provisional licence holder and have at least one rear seat and seat-belt fitted and in working order. There should be sufficient room for the SE to sit comfortably.

Some cars, although fitted with a rear seat do not provide sufficient space for a second passenger to be able to sit comfortably; **these vehicles are not acceptable for a Check Test**. If you have any doubts about whether the car you intend to bring is suitable or not, you should contact your local SE when you receive the invitation. Should your pupil decide to use their own car, a check on the state of that vehicle beforehand would be a sensible precaution. **Don't leave that check until the day of the Check Test.**

If you are charging for the lesson you must correctly display your ADI Certificate. Even if you are not charging for the lesson, you should bring the certificate with you for inspection.

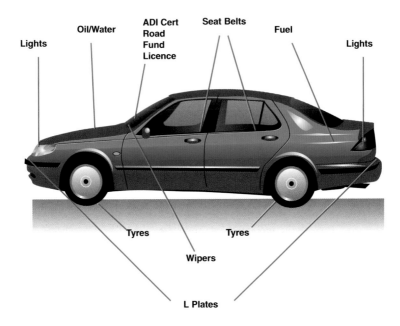

Lights   Oil/Water   ADI Cert Road Fund Licence   Seat Belts   Fuel   Lights

Tyres   Tyres

Wipers

L Plates

Failing to comply with these conditions will result in the test being cancelled and a further appointment being made at the earliest opportunity. **Persistent failure to present yourself for a Check Test in a suitable vehicle could leave you open to removal from the Register.**

The pupil

Your preparation for the check test lesson should really be no more, or less, than you would make for any other lesson. There is nothing wrong with using training aids if that is your usual method; but make sure they are ready and available when needed.

A very common mistake many ADIs make is to bring their 'star' pupil when attending for a Check Test. This is missing the point. **The SE wants to assess your ability to instruct, not your pupil's ability to drive.** What the SE will look for is your ability to give a lesson tailored to your pupil's level, whether a total novice, an 'experienced' learner or a full licence holder. It is also acceptable to give a Pass Plus lesson for a Check Test.

The lesson

The SE will expect you to give your pupil a lesson lasting 60 minutes, and then be available for about 15 minutes afterwards. This allows the SE time to give you a debrief of the lesson and tell you of the result. The SE may also offer help and/or advice on how to improve and/or up-date your instructional ability.

You should conduct the lesson in the way you normally would. There are two good reasons for this.

- If you try to put on an act, it may very well make your pupil feel uneasy.

- Changing your normal method of instruction, or attempting to be someone you are not, may be difficult to sustain for the hour. This could cause you to lose your concentration.

Experience has shown that many ADIs have misconceptions about what is required. Giving a Check Test lesson in any way other than your normal style would not be a true reflection of your competence. This may have an adverse effect on the overall assessment of your instructional ability.

Be yourself and have less to think about.

If there is anything incorrect or out-dated with your methods or instructional technique, the SE will do their best to help you put it right. SEs are not looking for the easiest way to remove you from the Register. The mutual aim of ADIs and SEs is to raise the standard of driver competence and encourage safe driving as a lifetime skill. This should be tackled as a team effort.

The two major reasons for conducting Check Tests are

- to ensure that acceptable standards of instruction are being maintained

and

- to give the SE an opportunity to offer advice and guidance on the way instruction can be improved.

Introduce your pupil to the SE in a relaxed manner. Tell them to drive, and to ask questions exactly as they would in a normal lesson. You should not imply that this lesson is different from any other.

As a professional instructor, you should have the skills and personal qualities to put your pupil at ease. Your pupil should be reassured that it is your ability as an ADI that is being checked and not **their** ability to drive.

How the pupil is treated and the ability to create a relaxed and friendly learning environment, is in the control of the person who is about to conduct the lesson. You should be aware that this is a consideration the SE will take into account in the overall assessment of the Check Test.

Normally, the SE will sit behind the pupil. This is because, in this position, the SE is best placed to observe the ADI's methods of instruction and control of the lesson and is less obtrusive to the pupil. There is also less need for movement to keep out of the pupil's line of vision should the lesson involve a reverse manoeuvre.

A reminder to the pupil at the beginning of the lesson that the car will be heavier with a third person in it, and how to deal with this, may be necessary.

The Check Test Marking Sheet – Form ADI 26 CT

This form is in two sections.
The top part of the form is the SE's 'Working Sheet'.

Here, the SE will record the following information

- the date of expiry of your ADI Certificate

- the name of your driving school or the name of the school you are connected with

- the make of car that has been provided for the lesson

- whether or not it has dual controls fitted

- whether the pupil you have brought is male or female

- if the pupil has been practicing privately or not

- the number of hours tuition the pupil has received from you

- the number of hours they may have received from another ADI.

WORKING SHEET

Cert. Expiry date [＿＿＿＿] SOM [＿＿＿＿] Vehicle [＿＿＿＿]

Dual Controls: Yes [ ] No [ ] Pupil: Male [ ] Female [ ] Practising Privately: Yes [ ] No [ ]

Hours of Tuition with this ADI [ ] Hours of Tuition with another ADI [ ] Role Play [ ]

Please circle main content of lesson: 1 2 3 4 5 6 7 8 9 10 11 12 13 14 15 16 17 18 19

Make sure that you have all of this information readily available when meeting the SE. If you take the trouble to keep written records of your pupil's progress (as you should), these and the details listed opposite, should provide the SE with a reasonable 'pen-picture' of your pupil and their present level of ability. You should also inform the SE of your intended lesson-plan.

Beneath this part of the form there is space for the SE to make any notes that could be of benefit as a reminder about occurrences during the lesson. They may be referred to by the SE when debriefing and/or offering you any necessary help and/or advice.

Below this space are the words: 'Please circle the main content of the lesson' followed by numbers from 1 to 19. The SE will complete this in conjunction with the markings which are recorded in Column A in the lower left part of the marking sheet.

The lower part of the mark-sheet is divided by a perforated line. At the end of the debrief following the lesson, the SE will tear off this section of the mark-sheet and give you the top copy. The second copy will be placed on your personal file which is kept in the SE's office.

Test of continued ability and fitness to give instruction (Check Test)
The examiner has marked each aspect of your performance in colums A & B below. See overleaf for explanatory notes

Instructor's Name		Grade	
Supervising Examiner's Name		Date	
SE Signature		P.Ref No.	

Column A   Column B

	1	2	3	Core Competencies	1	2	3		4	5	6
1. Controls				Fault identification							
2. Move away/stopping				Fault analysis							
3. Emergency stop				Remedial action							
4. Reverse left/right											
5. Turn in the road				Instructional techniques							
6. Reverse park				Recap at start							
7. Mirrors				Aims/Objectives							
8. Signals				Level of instruction							
9. Planning				Planning of lesson							
10. Use of speed				Control of lesson							
11. Junctions				Communication							
12. Roundabouts				Q & A Technique							
13. Meet/Cross/Overtake				Feedback/Encouragement							
14. Positioning				Instructor's use of controls							
15. Adequate clearance				Recap at end							
16. Pedestrian crossings											
17. Anticipation/Awareness											
18. Dual C'way/Motorway				Instructor characteristics							
19. Pass Plus Module				Attitude & approach to pupil							

ADI 26CT (A)   (Rev 7/98)

Column A is split into three sub-columns which are divided into boxes with the numbers 1, 2, 3 across the top of each sub-column.

To the left of Column A there is a list of subject items numbered 1 to 19.

The subject items are short descriptions that cover the topics an ADI may need to give instruction on.

Subject item numbers 4, 13, 17 and 18 categorise more than one subject. For example, number 4 lists Reverse left/right. The SE when marking column A, would delete the subject not applicable to the lesson. That is, if the lesson was to deal with the left reverse exercise, the SE would delete the word 'right'.

Most of the subject items are self-explanatory. However, the following are brief explanations of each.

Controls The theoretical and practical knowledge of safety aspects on entering the car and the correct use of all vehicle controls.

Moving away/stopping Theory and practice of taking proper precautions before moving off and stopping. Moving away smoothly under control and making normal stops using the MSM/PSL routine.

This includes moving off on the level, at an angle and up and downhill.

	Column A		
	1	2	3
1. Controls			
2. Move away/stopping			
3. Emergency stop			
4. Reverse left/right			
5. Turn in the road			
6. Reverse park			
7. Mirrors			
8. Signals			
9. Planning			
10. Use of speed			
11. Junctions			
12. Roundabouts			
13. Meet/Cross/Overtake			
14. Positioning			
15. Adequate clearance			
16. Pedestrian crossings			
17. Anticipation/Awareness			
18. Dual C'way/Motorway			
19. Pass Plus Module			

Emergency stop Covers all aspects of this exercise including skidding and varying road surfaces and weather conditions.

Reverse left/right Co-ordination of controls, observation and accuracy for both left and right corner exercises.

Turn in the road Co-ordination of controls, observation and accuracy.

Reverse park Co-ordination of controls, observation and accuracy.

Mirrors Teaching the subject as an integral part of driving routine. Must include the use of both interior and exterior mirrors where fitted.

Signals By indicators and arm, to include correct timing and unnecessary use of signals.

Planning Development of forward planning and hazard perception including the use of the MSM/PSL routine.

Use of speed Correct use of speed: making progress when safe to do so, too fast or slow for road and traffic conditions or approaching hazards, e.g., bends, speed limits, etc.

Junctions Includes junction procedure when turning left/right and going ahead. Covers all types of junctions including crossroads, T-junctions, box-junctions, etc.

Roundabouts Covers the procedure on approaching, entering, negotiating and exiting all types, including mini-roundabouts.

Meet/Cross/Overtake Developing sound judgement and awareness of priorities in varying road and traffic situations in relation to other road users.

Positioning This covers general positioning during normal driving, including lane discipline, one way systems and road markings.

Adequate clearance Developing awareness and sound judgement of how to approach and pass stationary vehicles safely.

Pedestrian crossings Covers all types of crossings, including controlled and uncontrolled.

Anticipation/Awareness Covers the actions of all other road users, including pedestrians and cyclists as well as other drivers.

Dual Carriageway/Motorway Comprehensive cover of these aspects, depending on licence entitlement, including varying speed limits.

Pass Plus Module Dealing with the topics as appropriate to the Pass Plus syllabus with a full licence holder.

The marking and assessment of Column A

The assessment and marking of Column A is the first thing the SE will take into account before arriving at the overall assessment of the Check Test.

Each aspect of the lesson content, whether satisfactory, unsatisfactory or not dealt with and should have been, will be assessed and marked under one of the boxes numbered 1, 2 and 3.

Box 1   Failing to identify faults that required instruction and guidance, or giving incorrect instruction, will be assessed as such and recorded by means of a diagonal line [/] in Box 1 against the appropriate subject heading or headings.

Box 2   If you identified a fault or faults, but the instruction offered was unsatisfactory or incomplete, the SE would record this with a diagonal line in Box 2 against the appropriate subject heading or headings.

Box 3   If the fault or faults against that subject heading are identified and correct instruction offered to prevent re-occurrence, the SE would record this as satisfactory by means of a diagonal line in Box 3.

The following scenario will show how the assessment and marking of Column A is recorded.

If your lesson-plan was to deal with meeting approaching traffic. The SE would assess the quality of your instruction on this subject.

A satisfactory assessment would be recorded by means of a diagonal line against the subject item number 13 'Meet/Cross/Overtake' in Box 3 and the words 'Cross' and 'Overtake' would be deleted.

If your instruction was unsatisfactory, the SE would record this by means of a diagonal line against the subject item in Box 2.

Should your pupil make persistent mistakes in other aspects of their driving whilst concentrating on the subject of meeting approaching traffic – for example, emerging at junctions – and you fail to address the problem, this will be recorded by means of a diagonal line in Box 1 against the subject item number 11 'Junctions'.

However, if you did address the fault but your instruction was incorrect, this would still be recorded with a diagonal line in Box 1 against the subject item number 11 'Junctions'.

It is most important that you continually re-assess the priorities of the lesson.

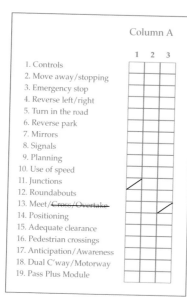

Column A

	1	2	3
1. Controls			
2. Move away/stopping			
3. Emergency stop			
4. Reverse left/right			
5. Turn in the road			
6. Reverse park			
7. Mirrors			
8. Signals			
9. Planning			
10. Use of speed			
11. Junctions			
12. Roundabouts			
13. Meet/~~Cross/Overtake~~			
14. Positioning			
15. Adequate clearance			
16. Pedestrian crossings			
17. Anticipation/Awareness			
18. Dual C'way/Motorway			
19. Pass Plus Module			

SE will expect this. Just because you have told the SE that your lesson-plan was to concentrate on 'meeting approaching traffic', does not mean correction of other aspects of the pupil's driving are to be ignored.

One of the most common errors ADIs make during a Check Test is sticking rigidly to the original lesson-plan when this is not the appropriate course to take. This will often result in a mismatch between the needs of the pupil and what is being taught.

Lessons should be tailored to meet the needs of the pupil. When errors in other aspects of the pupil's drive are identified, the correct response from a good ADI will be to assess the seriousness of them and adjust the lesson accordingly, even to the point of changing the lesson-plan to suit those needs.

In the scenario, although the original lesson-plan was to deal with meeting approaching traffic, a problem of emerging at junctions, although covered on previous lessons, has re-occurred.

Emerging safely and correctly at junctions is a more basic and fundamental problem than the more complicated subject of meeting approaching traffic.

You need to assess which of the subjects is now more important, then adjust the original lesson-plan to suit the needs of the pupil.

If the pupil's level of ability has taken a step backwards you must match this need by adjusting your instruction and the lesson-plan accordingly. The

The layout and explanation of Column B

Below the heading 'Column B' there is a six point rating scale, numbered 1–6.

The column is set out in three separate sections.

- Core competencies.
- Instructional techniques.
- Instructor characteristics.

These sections are broken down into specific subject items which, when individually assessed and marked, will reflect the strengths and/or weaknesses of an ADI's instructional ability.

The SE will insert your name, their name and signature, your Personal Reference Number (PRN), the date and, finally, the overall grading of the Check Test.

Test of continued ability and fitness to give instruction (Check Test)
The examiner has marked each aspect of your performance in colums A & B below. See overleaf for explanatory notes

Instructor's Name

Supervising Examiner's Name

SE Signature

Grade

Date

P.Ref No.

Column B

	1	2	3		4	5	6
Core Competencies							
Fault identification							
Fault analysis							
Remedial action							
Instructional techniques							
Recap at start							
Aims/Objectives							
Level of instruction							
Planning of lesson							
Control of lesson							
Communication							
Q & A Technique							
Feedback/Encouragement							
Instructor's use of controls							
Recap at end							
Instructor characteristics							
Attitude & approach to pupil							

As with Column A, the marks are recorded by means of a diagonal line [/] in the appropriate rating box. Ratings marked in Box 1 are the lowest attainment and those in Box 6 the highest. Boxes 1, 2 and 3 represent unsatisfactory ratings and Boxes 4, 5 and 6 satisfactory.

The markings in Column B reflect the overall performance in relation to

- core competencies
- instructional techniques
- instructor characteristics.

When marking Column B, the SE will assess the quality of instruction applicable to each subject item. A single mark is then recorded in one of the boxes under the appropriate rating number.

There is, however, one exception – the subject item 'Instructor's use of controls'. If the ADI does not use any of the controls and there was no need to, the rating scale would be ruled through with a single line as no assessment could be made.

	Column B					
	1	2	3	4	5	6
Core Competencies						
Fault identification						
Fault analysis						
Remedial action						
Instructional techniques						
Recap at start						
Aims/Objectives						
Level of instruction						
Planning of lesson						
Control of lesson						
Communication						
Q & A Technique						
Feedback/Encouragement						
Instructor's use of controls						
Recap at end						
Instructor characteristics						
Attitude & approach to pupil						

Core competencies

There are three core competencies that form the basis of good instruction.

- Fault identification.
- Fault analysis.
- Remedial action.

While waiting for faults to occur may be necessary, more benefit can be obtained by anticipating a pupil's actions and dealing with them positively in advance.

You must correctly identify, analyse and remedy weaknesses to improve a pupil's driving skills.

When giving instruction, a very simple method to apply is to ask yourself three questions

- **What** happened?
- **Why** did it happen?
- **How** do I put it right?

Then tell the pupil

- **what** happened
- **why** it happened
- **how** to put it right.

These questions are reflected in the three core competencies.

The pupil has just committed a fault. Has the ADI identified it?

Identification – What happened?

The SE will assess your ability to clearly identify, **at appropriate times,** all important weaknesses which may need further guidance. You must be able to prioritise and decide whether the fault was serious enough to bring to the pupil's attention at the time or was of a very minor and/or one-off nature not worthy of mention. This ability is expected to cover all aspects of car control and road procedure at all times.

You must switch between observation of the pupil and what is happening outside. This can be done directly by eye and with the use of strategically placed mirrors. Faults happen inside the car as well as outside.

Lack of effective fault identification in instructors is quite common. Often this is caused by giving instruction whilst looking through the windscreen.

For example, you have asked the pupil to move off from the side of the road when it is safe. Whilst making this request, you should be watching the pupil closely as well as checking that it is safe to proceed.

This is the only way you have of knowing if your pupil has followed the correct routine to move off.

Failing to confirm correct procedure can result in you demoralising your pupil by commenting on a non-existent fault, and would also be a missed opportunity to give praise.

Recognising faults is the very first step towards correction. You cannot possibly improve a pupil's ability if you are not watching – at the right time – what they are doing.

Watch the pupil and you will *identify* the fault.

Analysis – Why it happened

Faults in either procedure or control that have been identified and brought to the pupil's attention, must be analysed to see why they have occurred and/or what effect they could have on other road users.

For example, when making a left turn from a major into a minor road, the near-side rear wheel mounts the kerb.

There could be several reasons for this. The driver could be

- too close to the kerb on the approach
- turning the wheel to the left too soon.

You should use your skills as an ADI to analyse the cause correctly and explain what went wrong. Many instructors possess the ability to identify faults but fewer display the ability to analyse them correctly.

SEs often hear the instructor saying, 'You shouldn't do that, the pavement is for pedestrians – you could also damage the tyres and wheels'.

This does not tell the pupil why the fault has occurred, it only confirms that it has; it does not teach them. Analysis like this, given throughout the lesson, will be assessed as 'unsatisfactory'.

The pupil needs to know what went wrong and *why*.

Remedy – How to put it right

Having identified and analysed the fault, the pupil will now need to know how to avoid repeating it – the remedy.

Many ADIs consider that offering a verbal explanation is sufficient; in most cases, it's not. Driving is a practical skill and it is most important that any verbal remedy must be followed by sufficient practice wherever and whenever possible.

The remedy must be given at the earliest opportunity. You must explain how the fault can be corrected and what might have happened because of the pupil's actions. Your explanation must be concise and easily understood.

Following the explanation, you must consider consolidating the theory with practice. Avoid leaving it for any length of time, as it is unlikely that you will be able to rely on the pupil's memory of events. Late or retrospective instruction is of little value. The pupil must not be expected to have the detailed recall of an experienced driver.

The pupil needs to know *how* to put it right.

Instructional techniques

These are the 'tools' available to structure the lesson and ensure that it provides an opportunity for learning to take place.

Recap at start

At the start of the lesson an instructor should briefly recap on the points covered in the previous lesson. This should include a reminder of what was and was not achieved. This should help establish a base line for the current lesson.

Aims/objectives

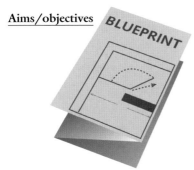

An 'aim' is the first step in planning. It relates to a general strategy and is a broad statement of intent. Aims are not full of specific details.

An 'objective' is clearly defined and describes exactly what a pupil is expected to achieve. All objectives should be 'SMART'

- Specific
- Measurable
- Attainable
- Relevant/realistic
- Time related.

Following on from the recap, clear aims and objectives should be agreed and set between you and the pupil. They should be matched to the pupil's ability and give a clear description of what's hoped to be achieved by the end of the lesson. This will help provide the pupil with a measure of their progress.

However, aims and/or objectives that may have been relevant at the start of the lesson should not be set in stone. If, during a lesson, the pupil does not show progress and begins to make errors that appeared to have been rectified in previous lessons, it is far better to deal with those faults than to stick rigidly to the original lesson plan.

You should not attempt to introduce or carry on with something new, when something dealt with earlier again shows weaknesses and requires attention. In this situation, you must change the lesson plan and explain the reasons why. Carrying on regardless with the original lesson plan, despite a change in the pupil's driving behaviour, is not meeting the needs of the pupil.

A good instructor will recognise the change and react accordingly.

Your aim should be to match the level of the lesson to your pupil's ability.

Level of instruction

This relates specifically to the match (or lack of it) between the level of your instruction, the level of ability of the pupil and also the area selected to practise.

Placing pupils into situations and/or areas of traffic which are beyond their capabilities will be assessed as poor instructional ability.

The effect of this type of poor planning could not only

- intimidate the pupil – and may even frighten them
- place them into situations far beyond their capabilities
- cause unnecessary frustration and hinderance to other road users

but, more importantly will

- compromise the safety of the pupil and other occupants of the vehicle
- endanger other road users
- bring into question your professionalism.

If an instructor has to make repeated use of any of the controls, it raises the question of whether the instructor should be dealing with that aspect of the syllabus at this stage as, clearly, the pupil is unable to cope.

It also brings into question the area and/or route the instructor has selected for the lesson. This is quite a common fault SEs see when conducting Check Tests.

For example, if a pupil is in the novice stage, it would be a mis-match between their level of ability and the area selected to take them on a busy dual-carriageway when they are only capable of handling speeds of up to 20mph in quiet suburban areas.

Surprisingly, some ADIs are of the opinion that the L plates give them the right and the protection to go where they want. **This is not so**, and displays an unprofessional and poorly-planned approach.

At the start of each lesson, you will need to judge effectively from your records and from the pupil's driving ability, at what level to pitch your instruction. For the levels to be well matched, you will need to identify areas of strengths and weaknesses.

It is pointless moving on and attempting to cover a new aspect of the syllabus if the pupil has not fully grasped or understood the previous one. It would also be wrong to hinder progress by not moving on if the pupil displayed sound knowledge, understanding and practical ability of the present subject. Failure to realise this will result in little learning or improvement in driving competence and this is not what effective driving tuition is all about.

When necessary, the lesson must be adjusted according to the pupils needs, i.e., to their weaknesses. You may even have to consider changing your original lesson plan to suit these needs. If this does become necessary, the pupil should be informed and given a clear explanation of why. The fact that you may have set out clear aims and objectives at the beginning of the lesson does not compel you to stick to them regardless.

The pupils level of ability will dictate the level of instruction required.

The art of successfully matching these levels lies in knowing when to instruct and when to stay quiet – so transferring the responsibility and decision-making to your pupil.

It is likely, in the novice and partly trained stages, or if the lesson is dealing with a new subject, that you will need to talk the pupil through each stage initially. When teaching a new skill using the 'talk through' method, it is important that the instruction is correct, concise and is given at the right level so that success is achieved at the first attempt.

When using this method, allow enough time for the pupil to interpret and carry out your instructions.

You should adjust the level and amount of instruction to suit the needs and ability of the pupil. If a fault remains evident despite attempts to correct it, you may need to consider adapting your method of instruction to suit the pupils level of understanding. Detailed instruction should decrease as the pupils level of ability increases.

There are several reasons why the level of instruction may not match the ability of the pupil. However, the two most common are

- over-instruction
- under-instruction.

Over-instruction If you never stop talking and telling the pupil what to do and how to do it, you will find it very difficult to assess

- how and what they are thinking
- their progress
- the effectiveness of your instruction.

Transferring the responsibility of problem solving and decision-making to the pupil should be done at the appropriate time. This will enable you to assess the effectiveness of your instruction and should help you identify what the pupil already knows and what they need to learn.

If, after several attempts to correct a fault, it remains evident, you may need seriously to consider changing your method of instruction. When one avenue of instructional technique fails to remedy a fault, you must consider an alternative method to achieve success.

Examples of over-instruction would be an ADI constantly telling a pupil whose ability was about driving test standard

- how to recognise the 'clutch biting point'
- how to brake
- when to change gear

at an elementary level.

Under-instruction Quite simply this means that instruction and/or guidance was needed but was incomplete. Identifying faults but failing to give analysis and/or remedial guidance is a prime example. Similarly, if the analysis and/or remedial guidance is incomplete, it is of little value.

In the example mentioned earlier where the rear wheel mounts the kerb when making a left turn, the ADI should

- inform the pupil that the fault has occurred
- analyse why and inform them of the possible effect on other road users
- give correct guidance to avoid it being repeated.

If there is a shortfall in any of these aspects, then the ADI has under-instructed.

Allowing a novice or partly-trained pupil to struggle through situations with little or no guidance is not good instruction and could be dangerous.

Saying very little and/or just listing faults and then pulling up at the side of the road to attempt to discuss them is of little value. You would be relying on the pupil's memory and powers of recall which may not be very good. This would be assessed as poor quality instruction as it is retrospective.

Planning

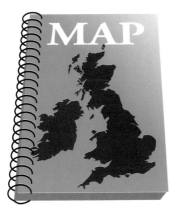

A lesson must have a start, a middle, and an end.

The lesson must be structured and presented in an orderly manner following a clear and logical pattern. You should take into account the complexity of the subject(s) to be covered and consider the allocation of time between theory and practice.

Briefings on new aspects must be planned and should be given close to, or at, the location where you intend to practice. For example, it would be of little value briefing the pupil about the turn-in-the-road exercise and then driving for some length of time before arriving at a suitable location to practice it.

A briefing must not be excessively long and drawn out. You must aim to cover the positive aspects, i.e., 'what to do', and avoid going too deeply into 'what not to do'. Involve your pupil and avoid presenting the brief in the form of a lecture.

You should avoid too much stationary instruction. There is only so much verbal information a pupil can absorb at any one time. Driving is a practical skill; they need to be *doing* as well as listening.

The lesson and your teaching methods should be linked to the pupil's ability.

Any visual aids, diagrams or reference material should be prepared (when possible) and close to hand ready to use. Avoid reading sections of text word for word. This would cast doubt on your knowledge of subject matter and also limits pupil involvement.

Failing to plan is planning to fail.

Control of the lesson

The SE will assess your awareness and perception of any changes, inside or outside the car. You must have the ability to anticipate and take appropriate action on any potential errors or dangers. This includes the ability to prioritise in different situations, particularly approaching and/or dealing with various hazards.

You must also display the ability to judge and assess the pupil's ability to identify or react to situations. When a hazard is identified you will need to judge whether the pupil is also aware and how they are likely to react.

The ability to prioritise is an essential element in controlling a lesson properly. It will be considered incorrect if you are still attempting to deal with an earlier hazard when the potential for another one is looming ahead.

For example, the pupil passes rather close to a parked vehicle.

Whilst giving the appropriate corrective instruction you are approaching on-coming traffic in a narrowing section of road (due to road works).

There is only enough room for one vehicle at a time to drive through safely, and you are now heading towards a non-existent gap and time is running out.

It should be obvious that the priority in this situation switches immediately from 'Passing stationary vehicles safely' to 'Meeting approaching traffic'. If you continue to instruct on how to pass stationary vehicles safely and ignore the approaching hazard you are not dealing with the priority at the time.

When you have dealt with the priority, you should return and complete your instruction on the previous subject or incident.

The SE will also be assessing your utilization of time between theory and practice and the allocation of time between stationary and on-the-move instruction, which should be relevant to the subject matter and the level of the pupil's ability.

The timing of your instruction is important. If you intervene too soon, you will not know whether or not the pupil was going to react or in what way. If you leave it late, the situation may become dangerous, and your instruction may become panicked and unclear.

The lesson is in your control.

Communication

Good communication is important if learning is to take place. You should avoid unnecessary use of jargon which may be confusing. If you do find it necessary to use jargon, make sure the pupil has understood.

Your delivery of instruction and correction should be fluent and straightforward, using simple terminology that is easy to understand. Give directions clearly avoiding any ambiguity or misunderstanding.

Be prepared to adapt and make adjustments to your style if you think the pupil does not understand you and avoid the use of superlatives such as 'fantastic', 'brilliant', 'absolutely splendid', 'mega', etc. They give a false representation of what has been achieved.

The question and answer (Q and A) session

The power of effective questioning as an aid to learning is sometimes overlooked. There are four reasons for asking questions.

- To motivate a pupil by gaining their interest and attention.

- To promote mental activity.

- To involve pupils as partners in the instructional process.

- To obtain feedback on the pupils recall, understanding and application of what they have learned.

It is a two-way process where the instructor may, at times, become the recipient of a question. Any questions or queries raised by the pupil should be fully and correctly answered. All pupils should be encouraged to ask questions or raise queries whenever they feel it necessary.

When considering the use of Q and A, you should judge whether the questions are appropriate in relation to the lesson, balancing the weight and complexity of the question to match the ability of the pupil. Make sure that the questions are testing and thought provoking.

Questions should be properly timed allowing the pupil to respond. Avoid questions about situations that have long since happened, as it is unlikely the pupil will remember in detail. This may be assessed as retrospective instruction which usually is of little value.

Types of questions to be considered

There are two types most frequently used which are defined as 'open' and 'closed'.

Closed questions   These are of limited value and can usually be answered with a single word.

There are two types of closed questions. Those that

- can be answered with either a 'yes' or a 'no', such as
  - can you drive?
  - is this your car?

- ask for a specific piece of information, such as
  - where do you work?
  - how many driving lessons have you had?

Asking questions that only require 'yes' or 'no' is unlikely to establish what the pupil is thinking or understands. Questions that ask for a specific piece of information are little more than a test of memory. Closed questions contribute very little to the learning process.

Open questions   These types of questions can be searching, thought provoking and challenging. They rarely limit the content of an answer.

To benefit both yourself, and your pupil, questions are of more value if they are formulated around the words 'what', 'why,' 'how', 'where', 'when' and 'who'.

Avoid using

• trick questions

• elliptical questions.

Trick questions usually show off the knowledge of the instructor and are of no value to the pupil.

Elliptical questions are those in which the pupil is meant to fill in the missing word(s). They can take the form of incomplete sentences. For example

Before you give a signal you should check the------------?

This type of question is of little use. It encourages single word replies and is more like a guessing game.

If the question is too involved or complicated it may cause confusion or distraction and may demoralise the pupil.

The Q and A technique, as with other instructional techniques, should be used when it is the most appropriate method of dealing with a problem and will enhance the pupils learning skills.

Overloading the pupil with a flood of questions is not good instruction. It can be very tiring and distracting.

Asking questions in hazardous situations to inexperienced pupils could be dangerous. They may find it difficult to concentrate on driving whilst thinking about the question. The question would, therefore, be of little instructional value – no matter how well it was phrased.

It must be said that in some circumstances **where it is appropriate**, it is possible to give a satisfactory lesson without employing this technique.

It is not the 'be all and end all' of giving instruction – as some people think.

Feedback and encouragement

These techniques can be very valuable instructional 'tools'. The SE will assess your ability to provide feedback and give encouragement during the lesson. Giving praise and encouragement can be a good confidence booster and enhance learning.

Feedback It's important to keep the pupil up-dated on their level of achievement. This will provide them with a measure of how they are progressing and keep them motivated.

Gaining feedback from the pupil is just as important as giving it. A good instructor will be able to recognise uncertainties or insecurities in the pupil through body language, facial expressions and/or the spoken word, and react positively.

Feedback from the pupil could come in the form of a question. You should respond with appropriate advice and guidance. Avoid ambiguous or confusing feedback which may not be understood. For example, if the pupil

asks 'Do I have priority at the next junction?' you need to establish why the pupil is uncertain.

If you just answer 'yes' or 'no', the only learning that will take place is that your pupil will now know that

- at that particular junction
- when approaching that particular direction

they either have or have not got priority. They need to understand **why**.

Encouragement In the novice or partly-trained stage, praise and encouragement may prove effective for the most elementary of achievements, whereas in the trained stage, praise for similar levels of achievement would be considered inappropriate and patronising.

Praise, when given, must truly reflect the performance level achieved and/or displayed. To say something was 'well done' or 'excellent' when in fact it was only satisfactory is not a true reflection of performance. Use simple and appropriate language: the use of superlatives, in most instances, exaggerates the true level of actual achievement and/or performance.

Instructor's use of controls

The instructor should only make use
of the controls to

- give a demonstration
- avoid a **potentially** dangerous
  situation
- avoid a situation involving
  actual danger.

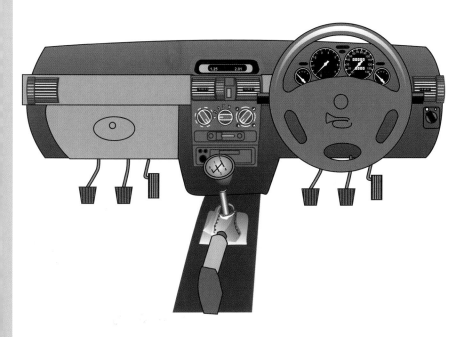

If it becomes necessary for the instructor to use any of the controls the pupil should be told why. This prevents the pupil from thinking that it was their actions alone that kept the situation under control. Use of the controls means *all* controls, such as

- the dual clutch, brake or accelerator (if fitted)
- the handbrake
- the gear selector
- the steering wheel
- the driver's sun-visor
- the wipers and washers
- the direction indicators
- the heaters, demisters and heated rear window
- the lights
- the horn
- the electric windows (if fitted).

If, for example, you are constantly switching the indicators on and off because the pupil has not remembered, it could be

- very distracting
- embarrassing for the 'pupil'
- creating a false sense of security – 'no need to remember those, the instructor will do them for me'.

It's important to ensure that the level of instruction matches the needs of the pupil to avoid unnecessary use of the controls by the instructor.

For example, if you ask the pupil to pull up at the side of the road and they misjudge the position on approach, and begin to steer on a collision course with the kerb, it is far more effective to react early by giving verbal instruction, than to suddenly grab the steering wheel or use the dual controls at the last moment.

A direct link regarding the overall assessment can be made between the subject items

- instructor's use of controls
- control of the lesson
- level of instruction.

There should be very little need for the instructor to use the controls or take physical action if the lesson is effectively under control, pitched at the correct level to match the pupil's ability and is practiced in an area suitable to meet the set aims and objectives.

If an instructor has to make repeated use of any of the controls, it raises the question of whether the instructor should be dealing with that aspect of the syllabus at this stage as, clearly, the pupil is unable to cope.

It could not only

- intimidate the pupil (and may even frighten them)
- place them into situations far beyond their capabilities
- cause unnecessary frustration and hindrance to other road users

but, most importantly, could also

- compromise the safety of the pupil and other occupants of the vehicle
- endanger other road users
- bring into question your professionalism.

If the instructor is controlling the lesson by using the controls, what is the pupil being taught?

Recap at the end

There should be a summary of the
main points covered during the
lesson. The pupil should be told the
objectives that were met and those
that require more practise. Praise
should be given for achievements.
Their strengths and weaknesses
should be identified and they should
be informed of the proposed content
of the next lesson.

Instructor characteristics

Attitude and approach to pupil

Last, but by no means least, it's vitally important that you create a friendly learning environment if you are to get the best from your pupil. If you have never met the person before, you must have the ability to recognise the type of person you are teaching and relate to them appropriately.

There should be no need for any physical contact other than shaking hands during introduction. Physical contact can be mis-construed and is often resented. Clear instruction will alleviate any need for it.

Patience and tact should be applied at all times. If the pupil does not get it right the first time, be prepared to repeat the instruction and practice, or look for the next opportunity to deal with that topic again.

How the pupil is treated and the ability to create a relaxed and friendly learning environment is in the control of the person who conducts the lesson.

The overall marking and assessment

The SE will assess your

- observation and proper correction of the pupil's errors
- method, clarity, adequacy and correctness of instruction
- manner, patience and tact in dealing with your pupil and your ability to inspire confidence.

You are in control of the lesson. It's conduct and to what degree it will benefit the pupil, depends **entirely** on your instructional ability.

The examiner marks each aspect of your performance in Columns A and B with one single diagonal line in the appropriate boxes. There are definite interlinks between the assessments recorded in both columns. The examiner will take this into consideration when arriving at the overall grade of the lesson.

The following is only **one** scenario exemplifying how these markings are inter-linked and the affects they have on the overall grading of a lesson.

Compare the following text with the graphic on the facing page, which is an example of the ADI 26 CT – the Check Test marking and assessment sheet.

For example, your lesson-plan may have been to introduce (or continue) practising roundabout procedure. However, if it became evident, in the first part of the lesson, that the use of mirrors and junction procedure – although covered on previous lessons – had deteriorated, a good instructor would recognise this and inform the pupil that it was necessary to change the lesson-plan in order to give further instruction and practice on the more basic procedures before moving onto, or continuing with, something more complicated.

Failing to recognise the need for this change and continuing to deal with roundabout procedure, would not be prioritising correctly for this lesson and, therefore, the instruction would not be properly directed towards the more basic needs of the pupil i.e., 'Junctions' and 'Mirrors'. It may also be placing them in situations beyond their ability and cause unnecessary hindrance and frustration to other road users. This is not good instructional practice and would be assessed accordingly.

The analysis and remedial action for *faults identified* during the lesson may have been quite satisfactory. However, it could be that a number of faults were either not identified or went uncorrected. In other words, the fault identification was weak.

The fault analysis and remedy were satisfactory on the faults that were identified and the examiner would record 'Satisfactory' grades against the core competencies 'Analysis', and 'Remedy' but an 'Unsatisfactory' grading against the core competence

Test of continued ability and fitness to give instruction (Check Test)
The examiner has marked each aspect of your performance in colums A & B below. See overleaf for explanatory notes

Instructor's Name _____ Grade **3**

Supervising Examiner's Name _____ Date _____

SE Signature _____ P.Ref No. _____

	Column A			Core Competencies		Column B				
	1	2	3		1	2	3	4	5	6
1. Controls				Fault identification						
2. Move away/stopping				Fault analysis						
3. Emergency stop				Remedial action						
4. Reverse left/right										
5. Turn in the road				**Instructional techniques**						
6. Reverse park				Recap at start						
7. Mirrors				Aims/Objectives						
8. Signals				Level of instruction						
9. Planning				Planning of lesson						
10. Use of speed				Control of lesson						
11. Junctions				Communication						
12. Roundabouts				Q & A Technique						
13. Meet/Cross/Overtake				Feedback/Encouragement						
14. Positioning				Instructor's use of controls						
15. Adequate clearance				Recap at end						
16. Pedestrian crossings										
17. Anticipation/Awareness				**Instructor characteristics**						
18. Dual C'way/Motorway				Attitude & approach to pupil						
19. Pass Plus Module										

'Identification'. This would reflect in 'Unsatisfactory' or 'Not covered' assessments of subject items in Column 'A'

7. Mirrors

11. Junctions

12. Roundabouts.

It would also reflect in the assessment of 'Instructional techniqes'.

Consider below the 'knock-on' effects and implications of weak 'Fault Identification'.

Aims and Objectives Assessed as 'unsatisfactory' as the main areas of weakness (mirror work and junction procedure) were not recognised as priorities. In this situation, the main aims and objectives should have been changed.

Level of instruction A lack of an ability to identify faults would result in a mismatch between the level of instruction and the level of the pupil's ability. Failure to identify faults would hinder a pupils progress as they would be unaware of their incorrect actions.

Planning How could the lesson be well planned to suit the needs of the pupil if the main areas of weakness were not addressed?

Control of the lesson The priority of mirror work and junction procedure required a more intensive level of correction and practice, which can only be instructor-led. Allowing a pupil to make mistakes such as these and failing to correct them is not retaining control of the lesson and could become dangerous. It will also result in very little improvement in the pupil's ability in these weak areas.

Feedback and encouragement This could be incorrect, incomplete or inaccurate as you were only partly aware of what was going on.

The recap at the start may have been very good, along with good communication skills and question and answer technique, but if you don't accurately highlight your pupil's strengths and weaknesses at the end of the lesson you will be assessed as 'Unsatisfactory'.

It can be seen in the above scenario, that, because of a weakness in ability to identify faults, there are knock-on effects on the ratings of other aspects that affect the overall assessment of instructional ability. In the scenario the lesson would have been assessed as sub-standard.

There are an infinite number of situations that result in different combinations of marking and assessment of these tests. No two tests are ever the same, simply because of the ever changing road and traffic situations and conditions.

For this reason, it would be rather futile to attempt to rehearse a lesson for the Check Test. This would entail using

- the same route, with
- identical weather conditions, using
- the same roads, with

- the same traffic conditions, at the
- same time of day, with
- the same pupil committing the same faults, in
- exactly the same places.

You must ask yourself if this is remotely possible.

If you want a true assessment of your instructional ability you must give a natural lesson.

Avoid acting. Conduct the lesson in the way you would normally.

The grading system

As previously stated your overall instructional ability is assessed and graded.

That grade achieved normally determines the maximum length of time between Check Tests.

After qualifying, the SE will normally try to conduct an educational visit within the first few months. The purpose of this visit is to give feedback to new ADIs in developing their skills. This is arranged and conducted as a normal Check Test. Where the SE is completely satisfied that the performance was competent, a grade will be awarded.

If your first Check Test appointment is beyond the 12 month period, you will have time to develop and gain instructional experience. In these circumstances you will be assessed according to the stated criteria and given the appropriate grade.

Registration is subject to the condition that an ADI will undergo a Check Test at any time required by the Registrar. Any just reason could bring the Check Test appointment forward.

For example, if the standard of your pupils being presented for the test is poor, the Registrar may order a Check Test at the earliest opportunity to assess your continuing ability to give instruction.

The following explanatory notes give the definitions of each satisfactory grade.

Grade 6

Overall performance is to a very high standard with no significant instructional weaknesses. Concise accurate recap given on the previous lesson and realistic, attainable objectives set for the current lesson. There was dialogue, with pupil involvement. Consistently demonstrated the ability to vary/select the most appropriate instructional techniques as necessary to suit the needs, aptitude and ability of the pupil. Quick to recognise and address all important driving faults and provided thoroughly sound analysis, with clear, prompt and appropriate remedial action. An appropriate route chosen for the pupil's ability and experience, taking every opportunity to develop the pupils driving skills and awareness using the problems presented en-route. Structured an appropriate learning environment that positively encouraged the pupil to develop further skills and good driving practice. The lesson concluded with a concise recap, which was an accurate overview of the lesson. The strengths and weaknesses in the pupil's performance were identified and discussed constructively. Realistic and appropriate objectives set for the next lesson. Professional attitude and approach to the pupil throughout the lesson.

Grade 5

A good overall standard of instruction with some minor weakness in instructional technique. A recap given on the previous lesson and objectives set for the current lesson, with pupil involvement. Demonstrated the ability to vary/select the most appropriate instructional techniques as necessary to suit the needs, aptitude and ability of the pupil, with only minor weaknesses. Recognised and addressed all important driving faults and provided sound analysis with appropriate remedial action. An appropriate route chosen for the pupil's ability and experience, taking advantage of most of the opportunities to develop the pupil's driving skills and awareness using the problems presented en-route. Structured an appropriate learning environment in which the pupil could readily further develop their skills and good driving practice. The lesson concluded with a concise recap, which was an accurate overview of the lesson. The strengths and weaknesses in the pupil's performance identified and discussed. Objectives set for the next lesson. Attitude and approach to the pupil was good throughout the lesson.

Grade 4

A competent overall performance with some minor deficiencies in instructional technique. Acceptable recap with limited pupil involvement and objectives for the current lesson outlined. Demonstrated the ability to vary/select the most appropriate instructional techniques as necessary to suit most of the needs, aptitude and ability of the pupil. Recognised and addressed the important driving faults, providing generally sound analysis and remedial action. An acceptable route chosen for the pupil's ability and experience, taking advantage of most of the opportunities to develop the pupil's driving skills and awareness using the problems presented en-route. Structured a generally appropriate learning environment that provided opportunities for the pupil to develop their skills and good driving practice. The lesson concluded with a general summary, giving an accurate overview of the lesson. The main strengths and weaknesses in the pupil's performance were identified. Attitude and approach to the pupil was acceptable throughout the lesson.

Grade 3

An inadequate overall performance with some deficiencies in instructional technique. Inadequate or sketchy recap on the previous lesson. Did not adequately set out/explain the objectives for the current lesson, and did not involve the pupil. Demonstrated only a limited ability to vary/select the most appropriate instructional techniques as necessary to suit the needs, aptitude and ability of the pupil. Inconsistent identification, analysis and remedial action of driving faults. Some unnecessary retrospective instruction. A poor route chosen for the pupil's ability and experience, missing opportunities to develop the pupil's driving skills and awareness using the problems presented en-route. Failed to structure a learning environment to enable the pupil to develop their skills and good driving practice. Inaccurate or incomplete summary at the end of the lesson. Many of the strengths and weaknesses in the pupil's performance not identified or treated superficially. Shortcomings in attitude and approach to the pupil.

Grade 2

A poor overall performance with numerous deficiencies in instructional technique. Little or no recap on previous lesson, failed to set objectives for the current lesson. Unable to vary/select instructional techniques as necessary to suit the needs, aptitude and ability of the pupil. Many problems with correct identification of driving faults and analysis, and very late remedial action. An unsuitable route chosen for the pupil's ability and experience, missing numerous opportunities to develop the pupils driving skills and awareness using the problems presented en-route. A poor learning environment from which the pupil would not be able to develop their skills and good driving practice. Superficial summary at the end of the lesson. Main strengths and weaknesses in the pupil's performance not mentioned. Serious shortcomings in attitude and approach to the pupil.

Grade 1

An extremely poor overall standard, with incorrect or even dangerous instruction. No recap on previous lesson; no objectives set for the current lesson. Unable to even recognise the need to vary/select the most appropriate instructional techniques as necessary to suit the needs, aptitude and ability of the pupil. Failed to identify, analyse or correct driving faults, many of which were serious or dangerous. Totally unsuitable route chosen for the pupil's ability and experience and did not use the opportunities presented en-route to develop the pupil's driving skills and awareness. No attempt to structure any kind of learning environment. No summary at the end of the lesson. Very serious shortcomings in attitude and approach to the pupil.

The next invitation for a Check Test will be as soon as possible and will be conducted by an Assistant Chief Driving Examiner (ACDE) or Area Operations Manager (AOM).

The overall grade awarded will be determined by the lowest rating achieved for any of the three core competences – identification, analysis and remedy of faults.

It must be emphasised that the grade achieved only relates to the lesson observed.

The result

The SE will inform you whether your instruction was of a satisfactory standard or not. You will be offered a de-brief on your overall performance out of earshot of your pupil.

Satisfactory

You will be informed of the grade you have achieved and have an opportunity to discuss relevant aspects observed during the Check Test. The SE will point out any areas of weakness observed during the lesson and offer advice on how to correct them. You will be offered a copy of the marking sheet which will record and confirm your grade.

Sub-standard

If the lesson is graded as sub-standard, the main points will be discussed and the SE will confirm them in writing. The SE will offer you guidance and advice on how to improve your standard of instruction. This is also your opportunity to ask any questions about driving and instructional matters.

You will be strongly advised to consider whether further training would help you to improve the quality of your instruction before your next check test. You will also be offered a copy of the mark sheet which will record and confirm your grade.

You will now be required to attend a further Check Test within the normal time limit depending on the grade. As a qualified ADI you must be fully aware of what is expected of you as a professional instructor, the need to constantly keep up to date with changes and the requirements of, and the necessity for, the Check Test.

Grade	Further appointment	Further sub-standard check test by SE
E	If in the first 12 mths and unsatisfactory re-visit by SE in 6 mths	Grades 1, 2 or 3 procedures apply.
3	In 12 weeks by SE	Written confirmation. Next visit by AOM or ACDE
2	In 8 weeks by SE	Written confirmation. Next visit by AOM or ACDE
1	No further visit by SE. HQ informed to be seen by AOM or ACDE	

Satisfactory Check Test by ACDE	Sub-standard Check Test by ACDE
Written confirmation. Re-instated into Check Test system	Written confirmation. Removal proceedings initiated
Written confirmation. Re-instated into Check Test system	Written confirmation. Removal proceedings initiated
Written confirmation. Re-instated into Check Test system	Written confirmation. Removal proceedings initiated

SECTION SIX | VOLUNTARY CODE OF PRACTICE

The topics covered

- Personal conduct
- Business dealings
- Advertising
- Conciliation

DSA and the driving instruction industry place great emphasis on professional standards and business ethics. The code of practice has been agreed between DSA and the main bodies representing ADIs.

It's a framework within which all instructors should operate.

Personal conduct

Being professional means acting in a manner that brings credit to the instructor personally and to the industry in general.

For example, an instructor should always be polite, punctual, give value for money and meet the legitimate expectations of the pupil. It means not openly discussing with others matters that a pupil has disclosed, whether in confidence or not.

It also means having a training vehicle which is properly maintained, roadworthy, legal for giving instruction and internally and externally clean.

As an instructor you should recognise that some pupils will feel threatened or insulted by over-familiar or crude language or behaviour. You should also recognise that some pupils, particularly women, will feel nervous about driving or being driven to lonely or isolated locations.

Priority should always be for the safety of the pupil, always taking every practical step to ensure that the pupil will feel at ease and secure in the learning environment.

Physical contact can be misconstrued. Except in an emergency an instructor should try to avoid it.

Instructors are free to choose their pupils. An unwillingness to give lessons should not give offence and the individual should have no reason to suppose any form of discrimination has been applied.

Business dealings

If money is taken in advance for lessons you should keep a proper customer account and the pupil should be kept advised of the state of their account. Money for a driving test application should normally be taken only at the time of, or immediately prior to, making the test booking.

You should explain the terms and conditions of contract before or during the first lesson, and you must provide a written copy.

A note of this action should be recorded. It must always be clear to pupils who have entered into a contract for instruction, whether they have a contract with the instructor personally or with a driving school. An instructor or driving school must ensure there is full compliance with the terms specified in the Consumer Contracts Regulations, and in particular with the unfair terms section.

It's unprofessional not to have checked a pupil's entitlement to drive or ability to read a number plate at the statutory distance. Failure to do so could leave the instructor open to criminal charges of 'aiding and abetting' under the Road Traffic Act. Similarly, it's unprofessional for an instructor to allow a pupil to arrive at a test centre without the correct documentation or, in the case of the practical driving test, in an unroadworthy vehicle so that the test cannot take place or has to be terminated.

The pupil's readiness for the driving test should be openly discussed and honest advice given. Should a pupil insist on taking the test against the instructor's advice he/she may wish to withhold use of the tuition vehicle. In those circumstances sufficient notice should be given so that the pupil will not forfeit the test fee.

At the commencement of intensive courses a pupil's attention should be drawn to the potential loss of fee if they are judged not ready by the instructor, and the fact should be recorded.

The pupil should be taught to drive safely as a life skill (not just to pass the driving test), with the instruction adapted to their needs. Driving tuition should be given on a wide variety of roads and in varying traffic conditions. Teaching on test routes alone should be avoided, as should conducting manoeuvres frequently in the same place. Care should be taken to avoid nuisance to local residents.

The whole of the paid lesson time should be given over to the pupil's instruction; none of it should be used for the instructor's personal business.

Advertising

All advertising should be honest and any claims made to such things as pass rates or Check Test grading should be verifiable. It's not uncommon for trading standards officers to prosecute for inaccurate and misleading claims. Both the Advertising Standards Authority and the Office of Fair Trading have powers to act against the publication of misleading advertisements.

If advertising pass rates is to have any meaning then it must be on a consistent basis across the industry. Records should be kept to substantiate any claims made.

Conciliation

Complaints are a fact of business life and the instructor should have a procedure for dealing with them which is open, honest and fair. Positively-handled complaints enhance customer loyalty; sensibly run businesses encourage customers to raise queries before they turn into complaints and correct mistakes before queries arrive.

The Registrar of Approved Driving Instructors is prepared to offer advice in an attempt to resolve a dispute.

As a last resort the Registrar will consider the setting up of a panel to advise on a dispute. The panel will contain at least one representative from the industry's Associations who are endorsing this Code and suitable persons independent of the driver training industry. Where contractual matters are at the basis of a complaint it may be a matter for the Small Claims Court or other statutory body such as a local authority Trading Standards Department.

Details of the panel and procedures can be obtained from

The ADI Registrar,
Driving Standards Agency,
Stanley House,
56 Talbot Street,
Nottingham
NG1 5GU.

The topics covered

- The right to appeal
- SE ADI offices
- Other useful addresses

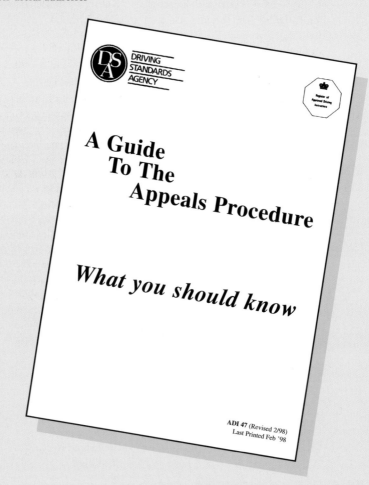

The right to appeal

The Road Traffic Act 1988 provides that any person who does not accept a decision made by the Registrar of Approved Driving Instructors may appeal to the Secretary of State in any of the following situations.

For those seeking to qualify as ADIs an appeal may be made when the Registrar has decided to

- refuse to accept an application for ADI registration

- refuse an application for a trainee licence or

- revoke a trainee licence.

For those on the Register, an appeal may be made when the Registrar has decided to

- refuse to retain a person's name on the Register

- remove a person's name from the Register.

Purpose of making an appeal

It's important to realise that in reaching a decision the Registrar will have considered your case carefully, and there will be good reasons to support his decision. The legal* right to appeal is there, in these particular situations, so that you can have that decision reviewed by an independent inquiry, called an Appeal Board.

You may feel that the Registrar was not aware of all the facts or had not fully taken account of all the circumstances. The appeal gives you, or someone you have asked to represent you, the chance to have your say and to submit any evidence that you feel will help to have your case re-considered.

> *   Section 131 of the Road Traffic Act 1988 ch. 52

If there are any matters you wish to query please write to

The ADI Registrar
Driving Standards Agency
Stanley House
Talbot Street
Nottingham
NG1 5GU.

Making an appeal

The process normally takes about three months. The procedure for conducting appeals is set out in legislation* and certain statutory limits have to be adhered to. You are therefore encouraged to read the following information carefully to ensure that you are familiar with what you have to do, and know what to expect.

---

*Motor Cars (Driving Instruction) (Appeals) Rules 1969, SI 86

Motor Cars (Driving Instruction) (Appeals) (Amendments) Rules 1970, SI 967.

The letter informing you of the ADI Registrar's decision, will say how long you have to make an appeal. Generally, you will have **28 days** from the date on the letter, but it is only 14 days if the decision is to do with the refusal or revocation of a Trainee Licence, so read the letter carefully.

If you wish to make an appeal you will need to write a letter stating

- the decision against which you are appealing
- the reason(s) for making an appeal.

You should include as much information as you can

- the address you want anything to do with the appeal to be sent, if different from your home address
- any inconvenient dates when you cannot attend an appeal hearing. Do remember to tell DSA if these change.

You are entitled to submit any additional evidence to support your case.

The address to send your appeal and any other papers relating to it is

ADI Appeals Section
Driving Standards Agency
Talbot Street
Nottingham
NG1 5GU.

You must ensure that the letter is received at the address above **within the time limit specified**, otherwise your appeal may not be accepted.

If you want more time to assemble your case, it's better to send a holding reply and follow that with a more detailed letter when you are able to. It's advisable to use Recorded Delivery in all your correspondence on the appeal, and to keep copies of everything you send, including your letters, as any of these documents may be referred to at the appeal hearing.

The Appeal Section at DSA works independently from the rest of the ADI Register. It's there to help you. Once the appeal process has started all correspondence should be addressed to it.

Remember to tell the Appeal Section of any changes that affect your appeal, e.g., if you are about to change address, or if you become unable to attend on certain dates. They are also there to answer any questions you may have about the appeals procedures. It is much better to get these sorted out before the hearing.

Please remember, you must give reasons why you are making an appeal against the Registrar's decision. If no reasons are given for the appeal **it may not be valid.**

Once your appeal has been received DSA will write to you.

- To acknowledge receipt of your appeal. If you do not receive this please contact them.

- To tell you the date, time and location of the appeal hearing and the names of the Board Members. You will be given at least 21 days notice of this date. Every reasonable effort will be made to keep down the cost of travelling.

- To provide you with the Registrar's Statement, which contains the reason(s) why he came to his decision. Attached to this will be all the documents that form part of the appeal case. These

will be sent to you within 14 days of the date of the letter informing you of the date, time and location of the appeal hearing.

Do I have to attend the Hearing?

It is generally in your interests to attend the hearing, so make every effort to attend if at all possible. You are entitled to arrange for someone to represent you. This may be a solicitor, a friend or anyone else you want to speak for you. If you don't attend and have not arranged for anyone to speak on your behalf, the Appeal Board may decide to hear the appeal in your absence.

In appeals concerning the Registrar's decision to refuse or revoke a trainee licence, you may prefer to have your case dealt with by way of 'written representation'. This means that there will be no formal hearing, but the Board will make a recommendation based on the documentary evidence available to them. You will save both yourself and the Registrar the time and expense of travelling to an inquiry if you agree to proceed in this way.

The appeal hearing

None of the Appeal Board members are employees of DSA or any government department. The inquiry may be conducted by up to three people who are specially appointed to hear the case. The Chairperson will always be selected from a list produced by the Lord Chancellor's Office, and the majority are solicitors, or magistrates, who have had many years of experience in the legal profession. The other Board members are persons of standing within the community.

The appeal is your opportunity to set before an independent inquiry the reasons why you disagree with the Registrar's decision. Your case might be made up of additional documents, letters, including personal testimonials, and you may feel that it would be beneficial to have your own witnesses with you on the day of the appeal.

The Registrar or the Board is also entitled to ask any person to attend as a witness or to produce documents, if they are relevant to the appeal.

If you employ a solicitor to represent you, he will advise you. However if you represent yourself, you may find it helpful to have a list of questions to ask, and the main points you want to make. You may also read out a statement you have prepared that sets out your reasons in a logical order.

It's important that you bring to the appeal your copy of all the documents the Registrar sends to you with his statement prior to the hearing, as these will be referred to during the hearing.

The appeal hearing won't be held in a Court of Law but in a room specially arranged for the purpose. The procedure at the hearing is less formal than a Magistrate's Court. Normally members of the public can attend if they wish, but either you or the Registrar can apply to the Appeal Board for all, or part of the hearing to be held in private. In practice, members of the public rarely attend.

Procedure Both you and the Registrar have the right to appear or be represented by legal counsel, a solicitor or by any other person. You will need to make it clear to the Board at the outset who is presenting your case. On rare occasions the Registrar may be represented by a barrister but in most cases the Registrar is represented by one of his staff who will introduce him/herself to you before the hearing commences, and will tell you about the procedures to be adopted. If necessary the Board will give guidance on procedure during the hearing. If you are in doubt about any aspect of the hearing it is best to ask straight away.

Presentation   The appeal hearing will generally start by the Board asking the Registrar's representative to outline the reasons for the Registrar's decision, and to call any witnesses. You, or your representative, are also entitled to make an opening statement, to call witnesses and to cross examine any witness called by the Registrar. The Registrar's representative may also cross examine you and any witness you call. At the end both you and the Registrar's representative will be asked to make a final statement. During this process the Appeal Board members may ask questions in order to obtain relevant information or clarify what has been said.

You and any witness may be invited by the Appeal Board to give any evidence presented at the hearing under oath, or affirmation.

Non-attendance   At any time before the hearing you can give notice that you wish to withdraw your appeal. However this must be made in writing, and once received no further action will be taken on your appeal, but you should be aware that in such circumstances the Registrar's decision would take immediate effect.

If you are unable to attend the hearing for any reason, you should let the Appeal Section know in good time. It will then be for the Board to decide whether or not to proceed, but they are unlikely to agree to postpone the hearing unless there are exceptional reasons.

If you do not withdraw your appeal and fail to attend the hearing and are not represented, the Board are empowered to

- proceed with the enquiry in your absence and make a recommendation based on the evidence available to them at the time, or

- adjourn the hearing until a later date or recommend that the appeal be dismissed through lack of evidence.

After the hearing

Every effort is made to ensure that you are informed of the decision as quickly as possible, and in most cases you will know the outcome within five weeks of the hearing date.

Recommendation   After the inquiry the Appeal Board will complete a written report which will contain details of their findings and any recommendations. This report will be sent to the Chief Executive of DSA, who will consider what the Appeal Board have said.

Decision   Under powers delegated by the Secretary of State, the Chief Executive has the authority to make decisions in any cases where there is no disagreement with the Appeal Board's recommendation.

If the Chief Executive cannot accept the Appeal Board's recommendation because it is contrary to law, illogical or not supported by the facts, he/she is required to refer the case, giving reasons for doing so, to the Minister, who will decide on behalf of the Secretary of State. This process happens infrequently, but does inevitably delay notice of the decision being given.

Once a decision is made, this will be conveyed to you by a letter, and a copy of the Appeal Board's report will be enclosed with it. Whatever the outcome of the appeal it will be confirmed by a written Order, a copy of which you will also receive.

The Appeal Board has the right to recommend that an unsuccessful appellant should not submit an application for registration or re-registration for a period of up to four years from the date of the order. The recommendation may be accepted in full or with modification and will be referred to in the written Order.

Your costs   Normally, you will be expected to bear the costs of any witness appearing on your behalf and any legal representation you may receive. In exceptional circumstances the Appeal Board may recommend that all or part of your costs are paid by the Secretary of State. If the recommendation is accepted this will be set out in the Decision Letter.

The Secretary of State's costs
These are normally met from public funds. However, if the Appeal Board conclude that your appeal has no merit or that you have not treated the process seriously, you may be required to pay all, or part of the costs, and these are recoverable as a debt to the Crown. In practice this only happens on rare occasions.

If you are still unhappy   The appeal process gives a legal right to have reviewed a decision that the ADI Registrar has made in certain specific situations

There is no provision in the Road Traffic Act 1988 for you to pursue your appeal if it is dismissed by the Secretary of State. If you are still aggrieved by the decision, you are advised to seek legal advice on what further action may be available to you.

Please remember, however, that the
Secretary of State cannot order the
ADI Registrar to do something that is
not permitted by the Act or by
Regulations.

SE ADI Offices

London and the South East

Driving Standards Agency
1 Coastguard Cottages
84 Wartling Road
Eastbourne
Sussex
BN22 7PT
01323 410348

Driving Standards Agency
Driving Test Centre
25 New Dover Road
Canterbury
CT13 3AS
01227 764577

Driving Standards Agency
89 Warley Hill
Brentwood
OM14 5JN
01277 217275 ('A')
01277 228412 ('B')

Driving Standards Agency
Driving Test Centre
Raydean House
15–17 Western Parade
Great North Road
Barnet
EN5 1AD
0181 447 0961

Driving Standards Agency
Milton Road Driving Test Centre
Wealdstone
Middlesex
HA1 1XQ
0181 861 5664

Driving Standards Agency
Fourways House
Rigby Lane
Swallowfield Way
Hayes
Middlesex
UB3 1ET
0181 813 6445 ('A')
0181 813 6447 ('B')

Driving Standards Agency
Crown Building
61 Lowfield Street
Dartford
DA1 1HP
01322 224520

Driving Standards Agency
45 Argyle Road
Sevenoaks
Kent
TN13 1HJ
01732 742265

Driving Standards Agency
134 Maple Road
Surbiton
KT6 4RP
0181 390 0801

Driving Standards Agency
Sutherland Lodge
St Omer Road
Guildford
GU1 2DB
01483 565993

Wales and Western

Driving Standards Agency
Valley Way Road
Llamsamlet
Swansea
SA6 8QP
01792 701176

Driving Standards Agency
Room 123
Bridge House Annex
Sion Place
Clifton
Bristol
BS8 4AR
01179 732161 ('A')
01179 732496 ('B')

Driving Standards Agency
Cook Way
Bindon Road Business Park
Taunton
Somerset
TA2 6BG
01823 271518

Driving Standards Agency
St Modwen House
Parkway Industrial Estate
Plymouth
PL6 8LH
01752 221824

Driving Standards Agency
Spur 4
2nd Entrance
GreenLane
Maybush
Southampton
SO1 9FP
01703 779285

Scotland

Driving Standards Agency
Driving Test Centre
2 Dunbar House
Balgownie Road
Bridge of Don
Aberdeen
AB2 8JS
01224 827246

Driving Standards Agency
Spur Z
Government Office Building
Sighthill Industrial Estate
Bankhead Avenue
Edinburgh
EH11 4AE
0131 458 5404 ('A')
0131 458 5306 ('B')

Driving Standards Agency
National Savings Bank
Boydstone Road
Cowglen
Glasgow
G58 15B
0141 649 0428 ('A')
0141 649 9927 ('B')

Northern

Driving Standards Agency
Block A
Spur J
Government Building
Kenton Lane
Kenton
Newcastle Upon Tyne
NE1 2YA
0191 286 5166 ('A')
0191 286 2236 ('B')

Driving Standards Agency
Driving Test Centre
1/17 Brus House
Thornaby
Cleveland
RS17 9ES
01642 769469

Driving Standards Agency
Woodside House
261 Low Lane
Horsforth
Leeds
LS18 5NY
01132 587987 ('A')
01132 582297 ('B')

Driving Standards Agency
Richmond Park Road
Handsworth
Sheffield
S13 8HT
01142 561127 ('A')
01142 449492 ('B')

Driving Standards Agency
Ashdon House
Cottam Lane
Preston
PR2 1JQ
01772 720629

Driving Standards Agency
Room 11, 1st Floor,
208 Drake Street
Rochdale
OL16 1UP
01706 354171 ('A')
01706 359026 ('A')

Driving Standards Agency
4 Mesnes Park Terrace
Wigan
GT Manchester
WN1 1SU
01942 826 604

Driving Standards Agency
36/38 Popular Grove
Sale
M33 2AY
0161 969 6633

Driving Standards Agency
Old Government Buiildings
Dee Hills Park
Chester
CH3 5AR
01244 320763

Midlands and Eastern

Driving Standards Agency
Ashland Street
Wolverhampton
WV3 0BX
01902 712938

Driving Standards Agency
Government Buildings
Clay Lane
South Yardly
B26 1EA
0121 764247

Driving Standards Agency
Shire Business Park
Stanier Road
Wardon
Worcester
01905 754201

Driving Standards Agency
Proctors Road (Off Outer Circle
Road)
Lincoln
LN2 4AL
01522 534343

Driving Standards Agency
Ordance Cottage
Sinfin Lane
Derby
DE2 1GL
01332 270116

Driving Standards Agency
Driving Test Centre
Tigers Road
Off Saffron Road
South Wigston
Leicester
LE18 4WS
01162 780791 ('A')
01162 780792 ('B')

Driving Standards Agency
Room G17
Government Building
Glastone Road
Northampton
NN5 7QG
01604 757454

Driving Standards Agency
Government Buildings
Jupiter Road
Hellesdon
Norwich
NR6 6SS
01603 429123

Driving Standards Agency
Henry Giles House
73/79 Chesterton Road
Cambridge
C84 3AP
01223 353320

Driving Standards Agency
6-10 Adelaide Street
Luton
LU1 5BT
01582 727281

Driving Standards Agency
Grange Way
Colchester
Essex
CO2 8HF
01206 865617

Other useful addresses

Driving Standards Agency HQ
Stanley House
56 Talbot Street
Nottingham
NG1 5GU
0115 901 2500

ADITE
Approved Driving Instructor Training
Establishments
PO Box 101
Stockport
SK4 4DW
0161 443 1611

DIA–RTE/DIA
Driving Instructors Association
Recommended ADI
Training Establishments
Safety House
Beddington Farm Road
Croydon
CR0 4XZ
0181 665 5151

Motor Schools Association
182A Heaton Moor Road
Stockport
SK4 4DU
0161 443 1611

Approved Driving Instructors'
National Joint Council
41 Edinburgh Road
Cambridge
CB4 1QR
01223 359079

AA The Driving School
Norfolk House
Priestly Road
Basingstoke
RG24 9NY
01256 493437

BSM
81/87 Hartfield Road
Wimbledon
London
SW19 3TJ
0181 540 8262

Driving Instructors' Scottish Council
67 Juniper Drive
Milton of Campsie
Glasgow
GL65 8HL
01360 312717

ADI Business Club
3 Greenacre Close
Wyke
Bradford
BD12 9DQ
01274 672850

Essential guidance from the Driving Standards Agency

New ways to take your test
Preview the theory test by telephone, online and on CD-ROM

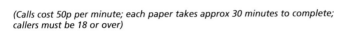

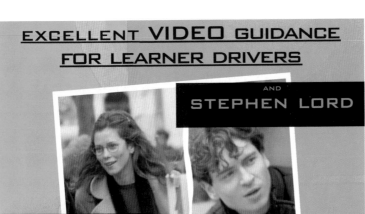

Essential reading from the **Driving Standards Agency**

Prepare for the driving tests wi

The Official Theory Test for Car Drivers & Motorcyclists (1998-99 edition)

Completely updated to include the new enlarged question bank (effective from end July 1998). Essential reading for all new learner drivers, this is the only official theory test title written and compiled by the DSA.

432 PAGES ILLUSTRATED IN FULL COLOUR
ISBN 0 11 552017 1
PAPERBACK   £11.99

The Highway Code (1998 edition)

The very latest edition of the definitive driving and road safety publication.

96 PAGES ILLUSTRATED IN FULL COLOUR
ISBN 0 11 551777 7
PAPERBACK   PRICE TO BE CONFIRMED

The Driving Test

Advice on the practical test - from the official syllabus, preparation, test requirements, skills to be acquired and faults to avoid.

90 PAGES ILLUSTRATED IN FULL COLOUR
ISBN 0 11 551778 2
PAPERBACK   £4.99

The Driving Manual

Covering everything that the driver needs to know about good driving techniques for today's challenging driving conditions.

336 PAGES ILLUSTRATED IN COLOUR
ISBN 0 11 551782 0
PAPERBACK   £12.99

Printed in The United Kingdom for The Stationery Office by MPS 86230   C15   03/02

e official guidance ...

Know Your Traffic Signs

The best selling booklet which aims to illustrate and explain the vast majority of traffic signs which any road user is likely to encounter.

100 PAGES ILLUSTRATED IN COLOUR
ISBN 0 11 551612 3
PAPERBACK   £2.50

Test Yourself Papers for the Driving Theory Test

Five practice papers for the theory test, with questions taken from the official question bank and the correct answers supplied for further reference and revision.

ISBN 0 11 551984 X
£4.99 (INC VAT)

The Official DSA Guide to Tractor & Specialist Vehicle Driving Tests

The essential guide for those who need to understand the principles of handling a tractor or special vehicle safely and your responsibilities to other road users. Whether driving the vehicle occasionally or regularly as part of your job the law requires you to understand safe vehicle handling.

96 PAGES ILLUSTRATED IN COLOUR
ISBN 0 11 552170 4
PAPERBACK   PRICE TO BE CONFIRMED

To receive details of the latest information on driving titles from The Stationery Office simply write to The Stationery Office, Books Marketing, Freepost KE5833 (No stamp required), NORWICH NR3 1BR, or fax to 01603 696784.